Resistance
✝Renewal

ANTHONY T. PADOVANO

Cover design
by Maureen M. Kane

All inquiries should be addressed to:

David A. Gawlik

CARITAS COMMUNICATIONS

5526 West Elmhurst Drive

Mequon, WI 53092-2010

262.242.5049…VOICE

262.242.7480…FAX

DGAWLIK@WI.RR.COM…EMAIL

Dedication

To the women who gave me life:

In memory (my mother, Mary)

In love (my wife, Theresa)

In hope (my daughter, Rosemarie)

In gratitude (my sister, Rose Marie)

Contents
Resistance and Renewal

Introduction

Writing is the most effective way of dialoguing with the human family across boundaries of space and time. These essays are efforts to enter the dialogue.

This is my third collection of essays. *Reform and Renewal* and *Hope is a Dialogue* preceded this publication. I have taken the liberty, in this book, to reprint in the "Milestones" section, the five essays which many consider the most successful of my writing career.

As in those previous books, the essays enter the field of controversy much more readily than the other two dozen books I have written. The longer volumes tend to be contemplative rather than conversational.

In any case, writing is a record of how some of us lived and thought. It becomes often a search for a truth we sometimes miss and occasionally encounter.

I offer these essays conscious that they are, at best, a partial picture of a larger truth we do not see readily in its comprehensiveness. Writing is not so much a celebration of what it is like to arrive but a report from somewhere on the journey that we are at least on the road. It is an act of hope that the path is right and the direction correct. It is an act of confidence that one's energy will hold out and that in the moments of exhaustion others will bring the message home and correct its ill-formed syllables.

Resistance

✝Renewal

1

RESISTANCE AND RENEWAL

Do we lose human rights when we accept baptism in the Catholic Church?

If this be true, the Catholic Church obstructs the proclamation of the Gospel and its own life.

The ministry question may be the clearest test case about the status of human rights for baptized Catholics.

I would like to address this topic in two parts. First, an historical reflection. Second, a discussion about ministry.

SPARTA AND CENTRALIZATION: A REFLECTION

As late as the sixth century B.C., Sparta created poetry and pottery of considerable merit. It was on its way to becoming a second Athens, an open, vibrant culture. Then something happened to turn it in another direction, against itself, so to speak. What happened to Sparta, then, is happening to the Catholic Church now. Allow me to explain.

First, Sparta. What happened?

The Spartans conquered a neighboring region of Greece, Messenia, and did something not done before in warfare. Until this time, armies fought in the field until one side prevailed. Then both negotiated the terms of settlement.

Sparta, however, chose not to negotiate but to occupy Messenia and turn its inhabitants into serfs. It decided to make Messenia Sparta.

There developed in Sparta a fear of those it controlled. Sparta, once open and creative, took now another path. It imposed on Messenia a harsh, structured, and unforgiving system.

It set in place, first, a rigid hierarchical order.

This led it to reject democracy and to prefer aristocratic government. To nurture this approach, it took young boys and raised them away from their families. Spartan art no longer depicted its earlier scenes of domestic happiness in which women were portrayed as the companions of men. As these boys became adults, they continued to live with their peers, dining with one another rather than with their marital families. They formed a culture of male bonding and of loyalty at all costs. They gave each other the title of "equals," and they called themselves "Sparteates." All others were called "inferiors." A system of rewards and punishments was put in place, so that a Sparteate would rather die than act against his brothers or lose his title and become an "inferior."

The second element in this system was the suppression of thought. It was not only external control but internal compliance Sparta wanted. The fear of alien ideas, of new and untraditional thinking, created a frenzy in Sparta. Sparta became more and more a closed society. It saw the outside world as an "inferior," not equal to Sparta, unworthy of teaching it something it did not already know.

The third element in the system was police surveillance. All "inferiors" had to be in their assigned places at all times. If they were not, Sparteates could execute them, especially if they wandered far from the farms they were working, or if they ventured onto the open roads or gathered in unwarranted numbers. The "equals," or Sparteates, were regularly on patrol, watching, accusing, terrorizing, killing.

In the sixth century, B.C., Sparta became a very different place. It had achieved good order and astonishing docility. It paid for this with the death of its own culture. It is not cited today by anyone as a culture of life or as a model for anything but tyranny. It became a culture of death.

ATHENS

By contract, Athens was unruly. It was fast becoming a democracy. It was chaotic. It favored open discussion, even criticism of its leaders. Sparta saw all this as decadence. Athens allowed choices and new thinking. Plato, in his *Republic*, suggests that women should become rulers, as well as men.

In the short run, Sparta prevailed. Sparta won the Peloponnesian War against Athens.

Such a victory! Who among us, today, if we had the choice, would choose Sparta? What lasting value did the titles and the bonding, the rewards and the punishments bring? Sparta created a culture of death, a culture that demanded the sacrifice of all that was deeply human, the sacrifice of thought and freedom and joy. Spartan culture expended enormous resources to maintain its artificial system and eventually became the victim of its own organized tyranny.

Who remembers Sparta anymore? It is Athens that won the minds and hearts of the world and changed the future for all of us.

Oppressive systems, secular or ecclesial, follow unerringly the Spartan model: hierarchy, thought control, surveillance. And they always lose.

We saw the same pattern, did we not, in the Soviet Union? That, too, became a culture of death.

I believe there were three great tyrannical regimens in the Catholic Church during the second millennium. They all eventually went the way of Sparta.

The first of these was the medieval papacy. Gregory VII, Innocent III, and Boniface VIII controlled the continent of Europe, its politics, economy, universities, monasteries, its cultural and religious life. Perhaps never before or since in human history did an institutional religious system control a continent so thoroughly.

The medieval papacy followed the model of Sparta, not the Gospel, but Sparta. It solidified the hierarchical system. It insisted on orthodoxy and punished deviant thinking.

It created a surveillance system of inquisitions, spies, and interrogation — indeed, of torture and public execution. How far from the Gospel! How close to Sparta!

The papacy did not gain the advantages it sought. The hierarchical system was challenged by the 15th century Council of Constance, and three popes were forced out of office. Suppression of thought became impossible after the printing press and the Reformation created a free exchange of ideas. Rome could censure books and condemn the Reformation, but it had no power to stop them. Surveillance of adversaries became counterproductive after the Enlightenment and the human rights revolutions in the United States and France.

The losses were so catastrophic that one would have thought the papacy would never again resort to such a model. It would have saved itself and many of us a great deal of grief if it had become a partner in dialogue with the modern world. It would also have influenced the modern world profoundly.

The papacy, seduced by power, preferred instead a monologue.

In the century from roughly 1850 to 1950, three popes named Pius (IX, X, XII) tried to control Catholic thinking, now that the world had gone its own way. They created a second tyrannical regime.

Two of these Popes issued the only papal definitions outside an Ecumenical Council in all Church history: Pius IX with the *Immaculate Conception* in 1854 and Pius XII with the *Assumption* in 1950. Pius IX, furthermore, pressured a Council, Vatican I, to declare him infallible (1870). The pope now emerged as the infallible head of a hierarchical order that would be the only reliable norm for Catholic thought and belief. *A Syllabus of Errors* (1864) and *Humani Generis* (1950), in effect, condemned the modern world, critical thinking, and contemporary theology.

There was yet lacking the surveillance system from the Spartan model. This was put in place by Pius X at the beginning of the 20th century. It was replete with codes, informers, oaths of loyalty, trials, psychological torture, and excommunication. It brought in a Kafkaesque world in which one never knew the accusers. The accused was presumed guilty. Interrogations were not public. No appeals were permitted. The condemned were not even told directly of their punishment. Rome dealt with the feudal lord (bishop or provincial), with the equal, or fellow Sparteate, and asked him to inform the vassal, the accused, the inferior, of the overlord's decision.

No advantages came from this century of oppression.

The Papal States were lost anyway. Both world and Catholic opinion eventually supported their loss. The items condemned by an ever–growing syllabus of errors were accepted by Catholics: the origin of the species, the structure of the universe, biblical criticism, liturgical reform, ecumenism, collegiality, academic freedom, the role of women, democracy, free markets, the reform of ministry, the centrality of Scripture. Now even a reactionary pope does what no modernist dared do a century ago. He prays in a mosque and visits Jewish synagogues; he apologizes for Catholic crimes and praises Luther.

All this happened not because the reactionary pope, John Paul II, or any of the Pius Popes had a wisdom the Church at large lacked. It happened precisely because the wisdom of the Church at large led the way in the Second Vatican Council. Sparta lost again, and Athens prevailed.

This second effort at ecclesial tyranny failed.

Incredibly, a third effort in this direction began with John Paul II. The issues are, of course, different. There is a call now for what no modernist endorsed a century ago: optional celibacy, the ordination of women, validation of some marriages after divorce, the acceptance of homosexual unions, limitations on papal power, ecumenical negotiation, and inter–religious agreement. Is there anyone who doubts that all these will come to pass?

The three efforts at ecclesial tyranny in the second millennium had different objectives. The medieval papacy tried to control the secular life of Europe and failed. The anti–modernist papacy sought to control Catholic thinking, and it failed. The reactionary papacy of John Paul II attempts to control the pastoral life of the Church. It, too, will fail.

Sparta won the Peloponnesian War, but it lost the future, the minds and hearts of people. John Paul II has won control of the Curia and the Episcopal College. He has lost the future. The Church is too big, the Spirit too free, the magnitude of creative thinking too expansive for one Pope or one tyranny to contain it.

A MINISTRY OF RESISTANCE AND RENEWAL

Until the Second Vatican Council, the Catholic Church had no substantive ministry of resistance and renewal. Such efforts, in the past, were rejected from the Church or left on their own. The emergence of a ministry of resistance and renewal is the legacy of the Second Vatican Council. And we are the heirs of this, sons and daughters of the Council, summoned to a ministry that is unique and noble. The Council clarified, and post–conciliar Catholicism has reinforced, the sense of a Church very different from the medieval and post–Reformation, Tridentine Church of the past. The Council showed us that Rome was closer to Sparta than to the Gospel. Indeed, the Gospel is against all the developments of the Spartan model: hierarchy, suppression of thought, surveillance, and interrogation. These features of Sparta and tyranny are at the core of the medieval papacy; they are essential policies of the anti–modernist popes and of the pontificate of John Paul II.

There is no hierarchical order, not even a Christian priesthood, in the New Testament. Even if one claims one can find some elements of the priesthood we have now in the New Testament, one must also observe that those elements might have developed in very different ways and that what we have now does not come from Christ but from our own institutional history. To read back into the New Testament a full justification for the priesthood we have now is to distort the text shamelessly.

There are varieties of ministries, certainly, in the New Testament, ministries from the Spirit, but ministries that can only be validated by the community's acceptance of them. There are no ministries of juridical moment approved by distant Church leaders who validate these ministries on their own and then impose them on the community. The New Testament sees this in the Roman Empire and rejects it.

The New Testament references are so abundant that we need not burden this essay with them. Everyone knows this who cares to know it.

Jesus asked the apostles never to lord it over others but to serve, without titles or phylacteries, washing one another's feet and choosing the lesser places at table.

Jesus did not promise the Spirit to a select few or to only one, but to all. Pentecost was not for a few priests but for the women and men, all of them, equally gathered in fear and longing. Pentecost helped them proclaim the Gospel; it did not endorse their superiority or teach them that they could dominate and terrify the community.

The New Testament was a call to freedom, not to privilege. It was a constitution for a community of brave and selfless people, not a charter for the suppression of thought, still less a handbook for surveillance and interrogation. A reminder of all this is what a ministry of resistance and renewal seeks to instill.

If anything were anathema to the New Testament Church, it would be a surveillance system in which victims were targeted secretly and relentlessly. One must not twist the New Testament call to accountability, or its fidelity to the apostolic witness of Christ's life, into an endorsement of a police force in the Church.

A secret and relentless surveillance system was anathema to the New Testament, because Jesus had been made the target of just such a system and had lost his life under it. During his trial, Jesus declared that he believed in open systems, since he had always taught openly in the Temple and in the market place.

A Good Shepherd does not have a spy system or encourage informers to come forward with anonymity. The Good Shepherd, quite simply, is not the Grand Inquisitor.

The New Testament has no place for a so–called judicial process in which people do not know their accusers, in which there is no right of appeal, in which the law is everything, and in which the law is heartlessly enforced. The New Testament has no place for this process, because so many Christians had been condemned to death by the Roman Empire, using just such a process. Many of our first century brothers and sisters gave their lives to give us a better model than that.

A ministry of resistance and renewal will not dishonor them by endorsing what a latter–day Roman Empire, headquartered not far from the Forum, across the Tiber, at the Vatican, gives us now.

We learned this, did we not, at the Second Vatican Council, during a new Pentecost, from a good shepherd and saint all the world knows as John XXIII. From that, and from him, a new ministry came into being. Its spirit is more important than its specifics.

It is a ministry of resistance against a Church that looks to Sparta rather than to the Gospel, to Caesar rather than to Christ. It is also a ministry of renewal for a Church desperately in need of freedom, starved for love, looking for life.

Should there not be a place for such a ministry? Is it not possible that we have been summoned to just such a task?

RENEWAL

We are somewhat clear now on what our ministry of resistance rejects. It rejects three features of Spartan life: hierarchy, thought control, surveillance.

There are three features of what a ministry of renewal intends: collegiality, biblical accountability, and human rights. I suggest that these features of renewal correspond to three great movements of reform in the second millennium.

It was the failure of collegiality that led the East to depart from Rome in the 11th century. It was the failure of biblical accountability that sparked the Reformation in the 16th century. It is the denial of human rights in the anti–modernist era and in the pontificate of John Paul II that makes the ministry of resistance and renewal so important for the future of the Church

I shall touch briefly on collegiality and biblical accountability, because I have already explored these themes at great length at conferences and in writing over the years. I will dwell longer on human rights and the ministry of renewal.

First, a brief word on collegiality.

A driving force in the departure of the East was the conviction that the Pope must not control the Church. One bishop cannot become the imperial overlord of a feudal system in which all others are vassals. If the Church depends for its life on only one bishop, then the Gospel has been lost and the community has been destroyed.

Indeed, the East insisted that no Pope or bishop could be above an Ecumenical Council.

The East has not become, in Orthodoxy, a perfect Church. Hardly that. Nor have we. But the East is absolutely right in insisting on collegiality.

I believe that John Paul II makes a grievous error in supposing that a Pope, indeed himself, can heal the divisions between Orthodoxy and Rome. No Pope can do this, since it is the very idea of a Pope who can speak, on his own authority, for everyone, without consultation and consensus, it is just such a Pope and a papacy, that led to the parting of the ways. Only an Ecumenical Council, a Council of free inquiry and free speech, a Council representing all of us, a Council conscious that it is above the Pope even though it seeks to be with him, only such a Council, only collegiality, can bring Orthodoxy and Rome together once more. It is not papal insignia but the gentle icons of a Church, not juridical but mystical, not judicial but liturgical, not dogmatic but spiritual, only these icons of Christ's presence can heal us.

Vatican II had it exactly right when it called for a Church of mystery and collegiality in its grand Constitution on the Church, *Lumen Gentium*. In the light of this collegial promise, episcopal synods were established, and Paul VI embraced Athenagoras in Jerusalem as a brother bishop. He did not embrace him as the imperial officer of a militant Church.

The violation of collegiality is a new Crusade by the West, aimed at the Orthodox East, seeking its compliance and submission to a Pope who is now more than the Pope of the 11th century was, a Pope who sees himself now as infallible, as able to proclaim dogma on his own initiative, claiming universal jurisdiction and supreme authority. Such a pope is not an icon of the Good Shepherd but an idol calling himself Vicar of Christ, a title the Popes assumed only after the East departed in the 11th century.

We, in a ministry of resistance and renewal, bear witness to the promise of collegiality, to the message of the Council. We do this, within the Church of Rome, not only because Rome deserves more than the papacy it now has but also on behalf of our Orthodox brothers and sisters, who will only stand with us when there is a collegial place for them and an honorable place for us.

BIBLICAL ACCOUNTABILITY

The Reformation was not about collegiality but about biblical accountability.

There was a sense in the 16th century that the Pope had made himself not just lord of the Church (as the East charged) but, worse, had made himself more than the New Testament. The *95 Theses* made this charge.

There can never be a harmony of Rome and the Reformation except in terms of Scripture. Just as the Pope makes reunion with the East more difficult by degrading all other bishops, so he makes reunion with the Reformation Churches more remote by putting on trial the theologians, Scripture scholars, and pastors who hold the Church energetically to biblical accountability.

The obedience of the Pope to the biblical norm must be clear before the Reformers will take their place with us.

Vatican II had it exactly right again, as it called for the priority of

Scripture in its grand *Constitution on Revelation*.

It is instructive that soon after the Council, Paul VI violated biblical norms on two crucial issues. Paul VI would not allow the Council to discuss mandatory celibacy or birth control. Neither of these issues is even remotely present in the New Testament. This does not mean, of course, that they must not be considered as Church policies, but it does mean that they cannot become Church teaching of major import.

Paul VI, on his own authority, without the Council and just after its close, in *Sacerdotalis Celibatus* (1967) on mandatory celibacy and, a year later, in *Humanae Vitae* on birth control, declared these policies authoritative Church teaching. Pope John Paul II has done more. He has made these policies normative for the appointment of all Church leaders and theologians. He has threatened and carried out the removal of bishops and theologians who do not teach them, or who even criticize them, or indeed seek to discuss them. One would think that these policies, coming late in Church history, had the same status as the creeds, or the cross, or the Resurrection or Pentecost.

One wonders how all this is made harmonious with the two great Constitutions from Vatican II we have cited already. It has little connection, I suggest, with the collegiality called for in the *Constitution on the Church* and makes no reference at all to the priority of Scripture proclaimed in the *Constitution on Revelation*.

I find it noteworthy that no Christian in all Church history has been called the anti–Christ more than the Pope. I, as a Catholic, certainly do not believe this. We are all the anti–Christ as we betray the Gospel. No one of us is blameless.

Yet I am intrigued. Why have so many Orthodox and Reformed Christians over the centuries called the Pope by this title?

I think it has something to do with the fact that the same Pope calls himself the Vicar of Christ. It also has something to do with making oneself more than the New Testament, not by explicit intent, surely, but by unintended consequences, at the least.

It does little good for the Pope to apologize for the violations of his predecessors. The indictment of his own behavior and the submission of his ministry, in a credible manner, to the collegiality of the Church and to the authority of Scripture, is required. Apologies with no amendment, we have been told, lead to no absolution.

A ministry of renewal seeks the human face of God. It brings us to terms with the sacred character of human life. It teaches us about God, not through exotic apparitions or distant places of pilgrimage, not in arcane rituals or juridical decisions, not in dogmas of questionable merits or in canonizations politically motivated, not in a blessing from a hierarchical officer or pope no less sinful than we, not even in sacrament, still less in an indulgence.

A ministry of renewal helps us discover, in our lives and in our personal histories, the incarnation of God's grace. It makes sacramental the names and faces of those we love; it gives liturgical resonance to the memories and griefs of those we have lost, and it finds revelation in our awareness of the false starts in our lives and the unexpected successes. A renewed ministry helps people make little of their sins and much of their hope. It finds God everywhere: in the way we feed our families and care for our parents, in the efforts we make to pursue our careers with decency and integrity, in the unspoken pain we feel about all we did not do or become, in the heartache we bear deep within us because the institutional Church so often substitutes anger for love.

A renewed ministry is passionate about human rights because every person has the right to be human.

The institutional Church's ministerial policy, I suggest, is the place where the human rights of believers are most outrageously denied.

The Pope and his episcopal collaborators have hounded tens of thousands of priests from the communities that wanted their ministry. Empty altars and ruined churches are mute testimony to a culture that is anti–life, a culture of death. The eucharistic malnourishment of God's People, the pastoral neglect coming from the absence of good priests and the presence of incompetent ones, all this makes it difficult to see Church leaders as shepherds, or as trustworthy. In the face of this, how can we believe the rhetoric that speaks of love as the abuse goes on, that asks for forgiveness even as the battering continues, that blames the victims for the crimes and the wounds and the cruelty?

The right to be married and the right to have children is not a crime. The right to one's good name and livelihood is not a sin. The right to speak in the Church and be respected is not an aberration. The right to a fair hearing is not misguided. The most fundamental human rights — which even dictators do not want to be caught denying — these rights have persistently been denied to priests and, of course, to others.

The People of God no longer want the priesthood they are being forced to accept. It is a stone, and they ask for bread.

It is simply not easy to find the human face of God in the Catholic Church.

The tenderness of Christ is so readily renounced in an appeal to use the power and authority of Jesus, as though the officer holder were himself the Son of God.

Without a ministry of resistance and renewal in the Church, we shall be led to settle for a God from Sparta, a Grand Inquisitor who is heartless and unapproachable.

Late in the deliberations of the Second Vatican Council, on the very eve of its closing, two mighty documents were proclaimed. One of these, the *Pastoral Constitution of the Church* (*Gaudium et Spes*), celebrated the human family for its goodness and its grace. It was optimistic about the value of humanity and eloquent in defense of human rights. A further document, the *Declaration on Religious Freedom* (*Dignitatis Humanae*), spoke resoundingly of conscience and subsidiarity, of tolerance and dialogue.

These are charter documents for the ministry of resistance and renewal.

The movement for human rights has all the attributes of a call from the Spirit. It is everywhere, and it is for everyone, and it is correct.

The last 50 years of the second millennium gave us the United Nations and the European Union, both with eloquent statements on human rights. We have seen the collapse of the Soviet Union and of the Berlin Wall because they were built on the denial of human rights. The civil rights movement and feminism, the end of colonialism, the sexual orientation revolution, all these derive from the belief that human beings have rights and that they are inalienable.

In the final decade of the 20th century, at Cairo and Beijing, the United Nations expanded its charter of human rights to include reproductive rights and concrete gender equality.

All this in the last 50 years. To this, we Catholics can proudly add the *Pastoral Constitution on the Church*, the *Declaration on Religious*

Freedom, and John XXIII's last will and testament, *Pacem in Terris*. We cannot add to this list the encyclicals of Paul VI on celibacy or on birth control. Nor do we add the policies of John Paul II. But what are these against the world consensus and the conviction of God's People that human rights are the shape hope takes in our time?

We are called to a grand ministry of resistance and renewal.

CONCLUSION

A ministry of resistance and renewal seeks the human face of God. This is what the Incarnation means, the discovery of the human face of God. We cannot find the humanity of God by denying people human rights. Or by assuming that people do not deserve them or will abuse them. People with human rights find God in the sacred places of their human experience. Thomas Merton once wrote: "I am in a condition of ecstasy over the human race." One can imagine God saying the same thing in the moment of Incarnation, or Christ proclaiming this on Easter morning.

We began this essay with a question. Do we lose human rights when we accept baptism in the Catholic Church?

We are prepared to answer this. Yes, we do, if we allow the institution and its approval to mean more to us than our baptism. The institution is least forgiving with those who do ministry in its name. It denies ministers human rights more regularly and more aggressively than all others.

We are not suggesting that ministers can do whatever they please. We do suggest that their human rights must never be violated.

Our response to the institutional invasion of our rights, of our conscience, of our dignity, of our calling, is a ministry of resistance and renewal.

We do not suggest that legitimate authority, or official teaching, or scrutiny of others, are always out of order. We do declare that the balance can be maintained only if collegiality, biblical accountability, and human rights are honored. All of these are presently denied by the Church of Rome. And so our ministry, in seeking to restore them, becomes a ministry not only of resistance but also of renewal. The agenda of collegiality, biblical accountability, and human rights is the legacy given us by the second millennium. We were taught this by Orthodoxy (collegiality), by the Reformers (biblical accountability), and by the modern era and its construction of a global community (human rights). All this gives us our charter for a ministry of the third millennium.

A ministry of resistance and renewal will not give the hierarchical system its obedience; it will not give the agents of thought control its silence or submission; it has no fear of papal inquisitors, curial spies, and pontifical police. A ministry of resistance and renewal simply denies to oppressors the obedience, submission, and fear on which they thrive. They shall not have that from us.

I am told that some of us are weary from the long struggle and discouraged from the supposed invincibility of the oppressors.

Yet the oppressors have lost their credibility and their power in all sectors of the Church except those few places where prelates have made an idol of what was meant to be an icon.

A revolution is not won in its early years, when the newness and the emotion carry us. It is won in the darkness, when we do not yield. It is not won in the springtime of its first appearance, but in surviving the winter of discontent. A revolution, in its early years, wins victories with cheap grace.

There were moments in the American Revolution, in the Gethsemane of Valley Forge, when the summer soldiers and the sunshine patriots left the field and returned to their farms.

There were moments in the Civil War when it seemed that this nation, and any nation conceived in liberty, could not long endure.

There were moments in Seneca Falls when women believed that their struggle to win the vote, and their decision to pursue this non–violently, would never prevail.

There were moments in Montgomery and in Selma when it seemed that America would always be half–slave and half–free, a house chaotically divided against itself.

Out of this season of despair, in every case, a few people — we know them by name: Washington and Lincoln, Elizabeth Cady Stanton and Martin Luther King — a few came foreward and refused to give the oppressors their obedience, their submission, their fear.

They knew, as do we, that their ministry of resistance and renewal, so to speak, had tapped a vein so deep in the human psyche that they could not lose. They knew that the oppressors had built a house on sand and that its future was temporary and its stability less secure than it seemed. We saw such a house in the Soviet Union. We see such a house in the Rome of John Paul II.

The glory of life is not in its easy first years; the greatness of a marriage requires more than courtship and honeymoon; the strength of any vocational commitment is not in its novitiate years.

Those who stay the course make the difference.

A ministry of resistance and renewal indicts the heart of darkness in the Church today. Its badge of courage is the light it brings, fearlessly, relentlessly, with no turning back and with no flicker of yielding, a light in a darkness so vast that it seems the light is pointless, even pathetic, perhaps unwanted.

We bear the light, nonetheless, because we know that even the darkness deserves a chance at redemption and forgiveness. We bear the light for the sake of those who come after us and deserve a better Church. We bear the light of freedom and human rights, the light of collegial companionship, the light of Gospel accountability.

We shall simply never give in. And we shall prevail. For Catholics at large have joined us, by their agreement with the issues for which we stand. The world at large will no longer abide monarchies with no collegial reference. Or authority with no accountability, or police states that violate human rights.

We shall prevail, even if we are sometimes defeated.

Athens lost a war to Sparta. The American Revolution was paralyzed at Valley Forge. The Union Armies lost the first day's battle at Gettysburg. Women were arrested for attempting to vote after Seneca Falls. Martin Luther King sensed his assassination in Memphis on the night before he died.

Lincoln was in office about the same amount of time that John XXIII was. Each of them reversed centuries of oppression. They did this because they went deeply into the tradition of their cultures, more deeply than the oppressors.

Yet the oppressors have lost their credibility and their power in all sectors of the Church except those few places where prelates have made an idol of what was meant to be an icon.

A revolution is not won in its early years when the newness and the emotion carry us. It is won in the darkness when we do not yield. It is not won in the springtime of its first appearance but in surviving the winter of discontent. A revolution, in its early years, wins victories with cheap grace.

There were moments in the American Revolution, in the Gethsemane of Valley Forge, when the summer soldiers and the sunshine patriots left the field and returned to their farms.

There were moments in the Civil War when it seemed that this nation and any nation conceived in liberty could not long endure.

There were moments in Seneca Falls when women believed that their struggle to win the vote and their decision to pursue this non-violently would never prevail.

There were moments in Montgomery and in Selma when it seemed that America would always be half slave and half free, a house chaotically divided against itself.

Out of this season of despair, in every case, a few people, we know them by name, Washington and Lincoln, Elizabeth Cady Stanton and Martin Luther King, a few came foreward and refused to give the oppressors their obedience, their submission, their fear.

They knew, as do we, that their ministry of resistance and renewal, so to speak, had tapped a vein so deep in the human psyche that they could not lose. They knew that the oppressors had built a house on sand and that its future was temporary and its stability less secure than it seemed. We saw such a house in the Soviet Union. We see such a house in the Rome of John Paul II.

The glory of life is not in its easy first years; the greatness of a marriage requires more than courtship and honeymoon; the strength of any vocational commitment is not in its novitiate years.

Those who stay the course make the difference.

A ministry of resistance and renewal indicts the heart of darkness in the Church today. Its badge of courage is the light it brings, fearlessly, relentlessly, with no turning back and with no flicker of yielding, a light in a darkness so vast that it seems the light is pointless, even pathetic, perhaps unwanted.

We bear the light, nonetheless, because we know that even the darkness deserves a chance at redemption and forgiveness. We bear the light for the sake of those who come after us and deserve a better Church. We, gathered here, so close to the Statue of Liberty, we bear the light of freedom and human rights, the light of collegial companionship, the light of Gospel accountability.

We shall simply never give in. And we shall prevail. For, Catholics at large have joined us by their agreement with the issues for which we stand. And the world at large will no longer abide monarchies with no collegial reference. Or authority with no accountability or police states which violate human rights.

We shall prevail even if we are sometimes defeated.

Athens lost a way to Sparta. The American Revolution was paralyzed at Valley Forge. The Union Armies lost the first day's battle at Gettysburg. Women were arrested for attempting to vote after Seneca Falls. Martin Luther King sensed his assassination in Memphis on the night before he died.

Lincoln was in office about the same amount of time that John XXIII was. Each of them reversed centuries of oppression. They did this because they went deeply into the tradition of their cultures, more deeply than the oppressors had. Lincoln went to the heart of the Constitution and John to the core of the Gospel. And, after them, no one was the same again. Even the oppressors were set free.

The sunshine patriots may need to leave us now. The summer soldiers may choose to abandon Gettysburg after the first day's defeat. A black American who makes it to the mountain top may find it a lonely place and see below all those who despaired of the summit.

All this is understandable and forgivable.

But it is not our road; it is not our journey; it is not our ministry; it is not our destiny; it is not our future. It is simply not for us.

We shall not barter our baptism with the loss of our rights. We shall not barter the Gospel with the Code of Canon Law. We shall not barter our conscience for hierarchical endorsement.

We shall not let weariness, so long our companion, become our master. We shall not let discouragement, so casual an ally, receive our loyalty. We have other dreams, better visions, more life, further light, wider hope, unshakable confidence and a measure of love that has a claim on us for as long as we live.

2

THE PAIN OF INCARNATION

Hope is the oxygen of the soul.

Many today are afflicted with fear and hopelessness and find it difficult to breathe in the Church. When one is suffocating, the struggle for air is agonizing. The freedom one feels as one breathes again is exhilarating. Air is such a striking image of grace.

How do we find air to breathe in the Church again?

This reflection is a tale of two Churches. Many of us have lived in both of them; all of us need to know what that was like. The fortified Church of the Counter–Reformation was very different from the pilgrim Church of the Catholic Renewal. In discerning the difference one learns how to survive and to serve and to breathe the air of freedom and peace.

THE CHURCH OF THE COUNTER–REFORMATION

We might date the Counter–Reformation from 1517 when Luther posted his ninety–five theses to 1962 when John XXIII opened the Second Vatican Council. We are speaking of a period which lasted for four and a half centuries.

One of the most telling features of this Church was massive building. We built with pride and prejudice, proud of the structures, prejudiced against all who were not Catholic. We thought we were building out of strength rather than fear but, indeed, fear was everywhere. One false step and we might not recover. What if we died before we got to confession? What if we fell in love with someone who was not Catholic?

What if we left ministry? What if our marriages did not last?

I remember clearly an incident from this period. A priest friend had died young, tragically. He was waked in Mass vestments. The mother of a priest who had left ministry entered the funeral parlor and there was an audible gasp in the room. The shame on all sides was painful. She was like a sinful woman entering the place where Jesus was but no one knew how to receive her as easily as Jesus would have. We simply did not know what to do. She sobbed at the casket in anguish and confusion and embarrassment and loss. She walked to the mother of the deceased priest and spoke in a voice that could be heard in the silence: "My heart aches for you. But at least your son died a priest. If only my son could be in Mass vestments! I would rather he were dead and a priest than to have him as he is now."

This woman, an innocent by–stander, and her son were outside the walls of the fortress we had built. There was no room for them inside. We blamed the priest for having done this to his mother. We found nothing in the Gospel or in the life of Jesus which could explain or justi-fy such a decision.

We went home and thanked God that we were not like him. We felt security and peace within the walls the Church had built around us.

In the movie, *Shawshank Redemption*, the prisoners identify with the massive walls which surround them. Eventually, they prefer the walls and cannot do without them. After release from prison, many become con-fused, depressed, suicidal.

We would not have been surprised if the priest who left the ministry had taken his own life. One understood such things then.

There were happy moments in the Church of the Counter–Reformation as long as one stayed within the walls. And there were holy moments. God pays no heed to walls and brings us grace wherever we are.

To be fair, one might even add that the walls served a purpose. If there were excesses in the Catholic system justifying a Reformation, there were excesses in the Reformation explaining a Counter– Refor-mation. If the assault by the Church on scientific inquiry was sometimes unrelenting, the scientific attack on religion was also unwarranted. And so walls were built.

The first tentative steps when the walls come down are unsettling and exhilarating all at once. It must have felt that way in the Exodus as the captives faced a limitless horizon and breathed hungrily the air of freedom. Not long after, however, the beleaguered community asked for the walls again and the chains and the slavery. Certitudes and walls can be comforting and, after a time, necessary. It is not that either is bad; it is the assumption that they are enough which is toxic.

Allow me to tell you another story. It is late January, 1959. We are in Rome. It is early morning at the North American College where American seminarians reside.

Later that year I shall be ordained a priest. The chartered Vatican City busses were ready, as they were on all school days, to drive us across the city to the Gregorian University. I was in third theology. A classmate shared a copy of the Rome newspaper, *Il Messagero*. I read the headlines: "At St. Paul's yesterday, the Pope Calls for An Ecumenical Council." I was stunned and confused.

We had been taught that there would never be another Ecumenical Council. Since the Vatican Council of 1870 had defined papal infallibility, there was no need to continue the cumbersome procedure of convening councils of all the world's bishops. Indeed, Pius XII had recently shown how this could be done, in 1950, when he defined the Assumption of Mary as Catholic dogma. Pius had surveyed the world's bishops in a process called "an ecumenical council in writing" and then created the definition in his own name. The era of the Ecumenical Council was, therefore, finished. It had stretched from the first Council at Nicaea, Turkey, in 325, to the Council at the Vatican in 1870.

There was another, more telling reason for my confusion, and this is the point of the story. I could not imagine why the Pope would call a Council. There were no overt critical problems to solve as had been the case in convening prior councils. The Church seemed to be powerful and successful by every institutional standard. In the United States, the Catholic Church had built an empire, almost a parallel nation, with schools and colleges and hospitals, with publishing houses and seminaries and cathedrals, with parishes and convents and orphanages. One could have all one's needs met in a Catholic ghetto of agencies and institutions. Vocations to religious life were massive. Men and women, lay and clerical, were obedient, loyal, and disciplined. So, what would a Council do? How could things improve?

Theologians speculated on what a Council might address but many did this to give the meeting an agenda so it would not be idle. Three issues surfaced. Mary would be given another title, Mediatrix of All Grace, perhaps even Co–Redeemer. Whether a bishop became successor of the apostles at his nomination or consecration could be precised. A fuller and harsher condemnation of Communism might be in order. The three issues centered on Mary, church authority, and adversaries. None of the issues had anything to do with Scripture unless one attempted a tortured exegesis. There was not a thought about lay concerns, liturgical reform, ecumenical unity, marriage, ministry, social justice, collegiality. Later, creative theologians and pastoral bishops would move the Council in this direction. They would be able to do this because the Pope, John XXIII, did not believe he knew more than the Church universal.

The vast majority of the Church expected the Council to be a large ceremonial assembly, colorful, innocuous, sentimental, pious, a retreat for the world–wide episcopate.

We felt no need for the Council because the system seemed to be working and an alternative to it was unthinkable. The system supported us, nourished us, made us part of something grand, divine, infallible, invincible.

The system worked, once we granted its assumptions and intent. To work it generated an illusion of perfection, sanitized history, idealized the papacy, demonized other Christians, subordinated women, exalted, in practice, law over Gospel, and created an aristocracy built on celibacy and clericalism.

We felt no need for change because the end result of the system was the Church as a splendid Temple, intoxicatingly beautiful, a Temple not in Jerusalem but in Rome. This was the Temple where God dwelt and we were God's favored people. Only here in this one Temple, with Rome's endorsement, could sacrifice be performed and the priesthood validated.

God had never been better served than by us in our Temple Church. To say that someone would destroy this Temple and build another in the Spirit was blasphemy. We would have died for this Temple, for its purity, its grace, its elegance, its truth. And we would have believed we were dying for God. For the Church had become almost a second Incarnation of God. God did nothing without the endorsement of the Catholic Church.

The Council, we reasoned, might be a ceremony staged within the Temple walls if the Pope felt a need for pageantry and display. Let the world see how great we are.

Allow me to bring the first half of this essay to a close with one more story, one everyone knows.

Jesus once took Peter, James and John to a high mountain, apart, by themselves. There they saw God in Jesus, transfigured, transformed, translucent. God was there, more beautiful than the Temple and with no need for it.

Peter sees Elijah, the prophet, and Moses, the law–giver and a Jesus who was different from the one he knew. His first instinct is to build something permanent, to preserve the moment and control it, a structure, a tabernacle, a temple for each of the three.

Peter was all of us in the Church of the Counter–Reformation. We were as strong as our structures then and we could not imagine God or Christ or the Spirit or ourselves without them.

The New Testament tells us that Peter was talking nonsense and he was talking that way because he was afraid. He had yet to learn that this Jesus of the transfiguration would do away with temples and reign from a cross; this Jesus of translucent glory would abolish structures and systems and find his place in the sanctuary of the human heart.

I left the Vatican City bus and entered the great lecture hall of the Gregorian University. The professor, a young German Jesuit priest, lectured in Latin about the Council the Pope had called a day ago. He informed us that John XXIII wanted to open a window and let fresh air into the Church. Hope is the oxygen of the soul. The Pope was ready to take down the walls and embrace all Christians and even Communists of good will. The Pope believed the Church did not have to be a Temple. It was enough if it were God's People.

John's Council destroyed the Temple in three years. God and truth and glory and grace had to be found not within the Temple precincts necessarily but wherever the Spirit led us. It would be difficult to leave the Temple and become a pilgrim. But for all those who began the journey, there would be no turning back. To turn back was not only impossible; it was not even desirable.

Without a sense of history, hope easily becomes fantasy.

We have surveyed the recent history. It is time to speak of hope and the troublesome issues which unsettle our souls.

I would like to explore four questions:

▶ Why has the resistance to reform been so strong and, one might say, so cruel?

▶ Will the opponents of reform prevail?

▶ How do we cope as we await the dawn of the new era we were promised?

▶ Is hope believable anymore or does realism require that we admit the dream has vanished, the vision has passed?

WHY THE RESISTANCE?

The resistance has been so virulent because the stakes are so high. We are not dealing with titles of Mary and condemnations of Communism. We did not realize fully in Vatican II that what started out as a ceremonial, polite Council escalated quickly to a reformation and a revolution. It challenged the system, its authority and power, at radical levels. When this was last done, four and a half centuries earlier during the Reformation, violence and bloodshed followed as people tried to recover what they lost or seize what they wanted.

It is ironic that Catholic reformers today feel hopeless. The strength of the resistance to reform is a sign of how deep the challenge is and of how successful it has been. It should not surprise us to discover that a powerful institution will resist as we question the way it has defined itself and exercised power for centuries. It will resist strongly if the critique is credible and if it feels threatened by the strength of the opposition.

The present reform movement seeks a change in the entire system, its structures, its sacramental norms, the papacy, sexual teaching, ministry, marriage, official policy, the way history has been written and the way the bible has been interpreted. The resistance is staunch because what is being dismantled is the Temple on which many depended for their life, their meaning, their encounter with God, their salvation.

There is fear, at times paranoid and hysterical but also pathetic, painful and understandable. Fear leads people to destroy what seems to be assaulting them. Was this not why Jesus was crucified? He took away the Temple and he also redefined power and sex and ministry and history and Scripture.

The first disciples felt some of the same fears the restorationists now experience. They rejected Easter in the beginning and believed in the cross and the tomb. The Church began with apostolic apostasy struggling to become apostolic faith. One can understand this. The new boundaries drawn by Easter abolished former certitudes and made impossible the Church of power and privilege the apostles preferred. There were tears for the lost securities, and frustration at the loss of a system of Judaism that was comfortable and secure. A generation after Easter, ongoing debate about abandoning Jewish practices is documented in the Acts of the Apostles. It was agonizing to leave the past and such a past.

Easter was as much agony as it was joy. The disciples did not proclaim Easter until pentecostal fire and the winds of hope sent them forth, with no endorsement from the past. Easter would not allow the disciples to build their faith around memories of all that was. It made it impossible for them to restore the past and fit Christ into it. Easter made Christian faith a restless, future–oriented experience.

Did we truly believe there would be no resistance to the reform called for by Vatican II? Did we suppose the resistance would not be massive, desperate, unrelenting? Are we not, however, unwilling to learn from history when we doubt the outcome? When people experience freedom, a freedom supported by persuasive ideas and structures which prevent anarchy, there is no turning back. This is why the Reformation succeeded and the Enlightenment and the American Revolution. This is why slavery ended and women were liberated and the Second Vatican Council prevailed. The Jews did not go back to Egypt and the disciples did not remain with the Temple and there is no one in the world, including those who first built it, who wish to construct the Berlin Wall again.

No return is possible for a number of reasons. The older system, as we have said, had good things in it. Many of its strategies and decisions were understandable. It brought faith and comfort. It might even have done what it needed to do for its own time in history.

But return is impossible, because three of the key elements needed to make the old system work no longer have the endorsement of the Church at large. These elements are belligerence, exclusion, and censorship.

A brief word about each of these is in order.

The old system needs belligerence to work. It was born in battle, in the wars of the Reformation, and it waged a cold war with its adversaries in the centuries after it was no longer acceptable to kill. The first draft drawn up for Vatican II by Cardinal Ottaviani and the Holy Office was called "*The Church Militant.*" It later became *Lumen Gentium*, "*A Light for the World.*" Such a gentle title! The old system used military metaphors readily. We became soldiers of Christ in Confirmation; marian apparitions at Fatima led to the creation of a blue army; we were an army of youth flying a banner of truth; the language with which we denounced Communism was the language we once used to justify wars and hostilities against Jews and Muslims, against other Christians and even the scientific establishment.

The unreformed system also requires exclusion and victimization on a large scale. For it to work again, women must become silent and theologians docile. Catholics must remain in marriages even when there is no meaning in them and priests must never fall in love. Protestants must be kept at a distance and the Pope must be seen as always wise and altruistic. Papal documents must be read more eagerly than Scripture and homosexuals must disappear. I suggest there is no longer the will, the heart, or the energy to recreate such a world of exclusion and subordination.

The unreformed system is invested heavily in censorship. When Teilhard de Chardin and John Courtney Murray were silenced in the 1950's, they stopped writing. Censorship was not only ordered by the institution; it was also self–imposed and the Church at large endorsed it.

Things are different now. No one of the major theologians censured by the Vatican in the last twenty years has stopped writing or lecturing. Indeed, the community at large has rushed to their side.

For the Counter–Reformation Church to prevail it must gain the support of Catholics at large for belligerence, exclusion and censorship. Indeed, in the strangest of ironies, those who resort to these means isolate themselves rather than their targets.

HOW DO WE COPE AS WE WAIT?

We cope by abandoning the Temple and the papacy as the substance of our hope. The restorationist agenda is exhausted and this must be dealt with whether the pope is liberal or conservative. Restoration simply cannot give life to the Church. That agenda requires high levels of theological ignorance and pastoral insensitivity for it to function.

We cope by stressing three values: our connections or faith, our need to belong, and our right to communion. A brief word about each of these may help.

We begin with our faith and our convictions. We must not be deluded into thinking that there is any future in the dull mediocrity of compliance we are being urged to accept. We believe in precisely the right things in affirming a reformed Church. It has about it all the logic of the Spirit. No other church can emerge from Vatican II than a reformed church. No other church has a future and no other church will have our allegiance and that of people at large.

The second of these strategies for survival is belonging. Isolation is terrifying. For this reason, small communities and our reform groups are healing, sacramental experiences. They bring us God and grace in relationship and community. This sense of belonging is essential, especially for Catholics, who find God in community more readily than in individualism. And so Call To Action and *CORPUS*, Women's Ordination Conference and Dignity, COR and We Are Church play a substantial role in our ecclesial, ministerial, and spiritual lives. Since the Temple is closed to us, and indeed, since its time is over, these small communities and reform groups are the synagogues of the renewal. In Jesus' time, synagogues were an addition or an alternative to the Temple. They gathered the laity and the marginalized and allowed the laity to preside at services. The synagogues outlasted the Temple, made the Diaspora possible, rescued Judaism and helped give birth to the new Church we call Christianity. Belonging is our baptismal and sacramental right. We must gather in the communities we require for our life. The institutional Church which created this crisis is not likely to solve it if we take no action. Edward Schillebeeckx reminds us of that.

The third strategy for survival is communion. By communion I mean a relationship to the Gospel, the Tradition of the Church and the sacraments. We need to enter into communion with all three. All are inconnected. The Gospel becomes more urgent for us as the Temple is destroyed; the Tradition becomes the way we struggle together to preserve and hand on the Gospel; and the sacraments assure us we are fully the Church. Every Christian Community has the right to the Gospel, the Tradition and the sacraments it requires for its life. This is especially true because the Church's law is always less than its life.

We cope, then, by faith, by belonging, by communion.

IS HOPE BELIEVABLE ANYMORE?

One must be concrete here.

There are only two Churches to believe in and work for: the Church of the Counter–Reformation and the Church of Catholic Renewal.

Do we really believe that there is a future for a Church which seeks to return to the past and, indeed, does not have the supports of the past? If this Church of the past were so right, why did people abandon it so readily and why did an Ecumenical Council fail to endorse it as it was?

History is a guide here once again. Nations do not return to monarchies once they create democracies; slaves do not seek their former masters once they are liberated; Egypt had no appeal for Israel after the Promised Land; the former Soviet Union has no allies seeking to reconstitute it.

In our Church the reformers are in the overwhelming majority. The reform is endorsed on the highest levels of biblical, pastoral and theological studies. What holds us back may be ourselves, for the most part. Our faith in our own cause weakens; our bonds of belonging are not always strengthened; and we lose communion with the Gospel, Tradition and the sacramental life.

The Church of the Counter–Reformation was a Temple Church, a

Palm Sunday Church, glorious, awesome, beautiful, elegant. But a Temple Church is an anachronism after the missionary journeys of Paul. A Temple Church can never be a truly Catholic Church since it excludes so many and confines God so much. And Palm Sunday is nothing compared to Easter and Pentecost.

Let me conclude by returning to Peter. We last saw him on the Mount of Transfiguration, eager to build monuments and cathedrals. We see him for the last time in John's Gospel, back in Galilee, with James and John once again his companions. Easter has already touched their lives.

Peter and the others are fishing and there on the shore, in the shadows of dawn, is the Risen Christ. Peter rushes into the water desperately, touchingly. He comes near Christ and he is filled with unasked questions. Who are you? You are not the same as once I knew you and yet I know it is you. Once before you seemed so different, on the mountain a year ago when we were with you. And yet I knew then it was you and I know you now. It is good to be here as it was then.

Peter has questions because Christ is not a Temple, recognizable, unmistakable, predictable, stationary. It take more faith and hope to be loyal to such a Christ. But the consequence of such loyalty is an Easter faith.

Peter is silent, looking for signs that his faith is not misplaced, his hope in vain, his love wasted. Christ breaks bread for Peter and painful, soaring memories rush in and carry him to the past. Christ, however urges him down new roads to the future. You must go, Peter, not where you choose. You must follow me, not your own preferences. I have but one question to ask you and if you answer it rightly you will always be safe and you will never be lost. You don't need a Temple now, only a mission.

"Peter, do you love me?"

"Yes, you know that, you most of all."

It is Peter now who is transfigured and who becomes the herald of Easter glory and a martyr for a Church of the future in a land not his own, far from Jerusalem and the Temple but not far from Christ.

This is the Church Tradition Peter leaves us, not an office in the Church or the papacy as an institution but love in a person rather than a Temple, the kind of love that always leads us into the future unafraid while bringing us out of the past unharmed.

And so this has been a tale of two Churches. Because I have lived in this new Church, I would know now what to do for the woman whose heart was broken by her son's abandonment of ministry. I would also know what to do for him. For the new Church has room for both of them.

Because I have lived in this new Church I will no longer be confused by a call for a new Council and I shall not assume we have no needs.

The pain is worth it. Every step of the way. Who would ever go back? Only the terrified and the frightened. My heart goes out to them but we cannot heal them by returning to the dead past, the confining Temple, the rigid certitudes fashioned from fears and insecurities.

We lost a Church along the way, a Temple of rare beauty, a fortress, a buttress. But we did not lose God.

The pain we feel now is the pain of Incarnation.

We trivialize that Incarnation when we make God into a Church system or a Temple or a Code of Law. This is too easy an Incarnation. It is much more painful and substantial for the Incarnation to take place in human life and for God's People to be the only Temple we have. God makes a covenant with human hearts, not with institutions. The Incarnation into human life is a crucifixion but its end result is Easter glory. The reform of Vatican II seeks to make the Incarnation, not a Temple reality but a human one, an Incarnation of God's Presence in human life itself. And this is a painful process.

For Vatican II, the Church is not the Church Militant or a perfect society; the Church is a Mystery, a pilgrimage; it is the People of God.

We lost a Church along the way but found a family. It is a family composed of friends but also former enemies. It is made up of those we once excluded and of those who embarrassed us and made our institutional life difficult.

The Risen Christ is always on the shore of our future hopes, in the gathering light where we are invited to come with fewer certitudes but deeper loyalties.

We lost an older version of Church along the way and entered into the turbulent life of a family where bread is broken and needs are diverse and exclusions are simply not allowed and loyalty to one another counts for much more than agreement with one another. In the midst of a family's fears and guesses and hopes and piece–meal lives Christ appears on the shore of its future. A family does not have the elegance of a Temple. It has something more. It is alive. A family lives by its answer to one fundamental question, a question once asked of Peter: Do you love me? The way we answer that question determines whether we have a Temple or a Church, whether we have an institution or an incarnation.

3

AMBIGUOUS VICTORIES

In the last five hundred years there have been three massive efforts to reform the Catholic Church. The Church is always in need of reform.

These efforts succeeded, I believe, but on a schedule no one preferred and with suffering no one wanted.

Some might question whether the reforms succeeded. The successes were ambiguous.

Indeed, ambiguous successes may be the most enduring.

REFORMATION

The first of these reforms was the Reformation. In a sense, it is the most comprehensive reform ever attempted in Catholic Church history. Its sweep, in retrospect, was breath–taking. There will be nothing like it until the Second Vatican Council some five centuries later. This Council, however, will complete the Reformation rather than starting out in an equally radical path. In actual fact, the reformations of the last five hundred years seek to reverse the medievalism put in place during the first five hundred years of this millennium. This medievalism gave us a Church of law and authoritarianism, of feudal obligations (such as celibacy) and of imperial prohibitions (such as the denial of divorce).

In the first five hundred years of the millennium a Church of external structures and canons was put in place. Not only this, of course, but it was a Church preoccupied with power and empire. The second five hundred years were a search for interiority, a yearning for God in the depths of the soul rather than in the alignment of the self with the institution. Not only this, of course. But the anxiety of the first five hundred years was for justification in terms of the Church. In the second five hundred years it was for justification in terms of God. The first five hundred years were less lonely but also less free.

Let us, however, return to our initial point.

The Reformation was formed in the cauldron of Martin Luther's agitation for God and on the anvil of substantial failure in papal leadership of the Church. It is difficult for us to realize how little spirituality mattered to the papacy of the first five hundred years of the millennium and of how much the raw politics of military alliance, money and monarchs dominated papal thinking. Luther's Reformation will impose on the papacy a need for, at the very least, the appearance of a spiritual papacy.

Luther's anxieties had less to do with reform of the Church than with finding God's approval and the serenity of soul that would follow from that. In this, he was a thoroughly modern person at odds with a fundamentally medieval Church. God meant more to Luther than his own suffering, more than the Church itself.

Luther, of course, did not go about his task blamelessly. Nor did Rome. There is no need here for the simplicities of saints and villains.

The Reformers, including not only Luther but Calvin and Zwingli and a host of others, believed that God would be more accessible if the Church were less intrusive. This too is a modern theme. Eventually, however, the Reformers created intrusive churches of their own and literal readings of the Bible which made it a paper pope.

Yet the Reformation was a singular grace for Christianity although people of the time demonized it. Like all grace, the Reformation coexisted with sin and, like all grace, it brought suffering to those it saved.

Reformations are driven less by choice than it seems. Circumstances demand a reformation and enlist frequently unwilling participants. Had it not been Martin Luther it would have been someone else. But it could no longer be nobody. The distortions in the Church were too twisted for the Spirit to breathe freely through them. The Church was suffocating for lack of life.

Those who reject reformers mistakenly believe that a few people are responsible. They assume that the following a reformer gathers is due to the reformer's charism alone and to the pleasure–hungry and ignorant masses. When reformations enlist overwhelming numbers and employ convincing theology and create, in effect, an alternative Church, these reformations are guided by destiny rather than misguided by dissenters. When the official Church resists them, it loses.

The Reformation was successful because it targeted the right issues: God over Church, Gospel over law, pastoral care over papal control, grace over sacraments, faith over works. It failed at those points where it became an alternative infallibility and when it began to demonize: papacy and tradition, celibacy and good deeds, sacraments and structure.

The road to reform, then, was arduous and ambiguous. It gave us a divided Church with all the acrimony and lost life divisions frequently bring with them. It is not easy to be inclusive.

Granting the scandalous and corrupt failure of papal leadership in the two centuries preceding the Reformation, granting the greed of the Avignon papacy and the deadly sins of popes fighting each other for legitimacy, granting the lust of the Renaissance papacy and the deceit of popes who made not only women but the Church itself their concubine, granting all this, the Church of Christ was weary and angry, longing for purity, starved for the Gospel, spiritually malnourished, ecclesiastically abused.

Looking back five hundred years one is astonished at the blindness of Rome's unwillingness to accommodate some of Luther's reforms. Erasmus had it right at the time when he wrote in praise of folly. Barbara Tuchman has it right now when she calls it a march of folly.

In 1520, merely three years into the Reformation, Philip Melanethon, Luther's close colleague, signaled Rome that reconciliation was possible if Rome would agree to two reforms, both of them canonized in the New Testament: a married priesthood and communion for the laity in bread and wine. A celibate clergy and communion in bread alone were seen as papal intrusions into the intimate life and sacramental rights of God's People. Luther wanted no new Church and said explicitly that he would never become a Lutheran.

Had the papacy responded favorably, half a millennium of division and bloodshed would have been avoided. Perhaps the most grievous wound the Church sustained in all its history was self–inflicted. Five hundred years after Luther the Church would praise married priests of the Eastern Church, multiply exceptions to mandatory celibacy in the

Western Church and invite the laity at communion to take and drink as well as to take and eat.

Some ten years after the 1520 overture, Melancthon, still a Catholic, drew up the *Augsburg Confession*. The Confession became the organizing charter for the Lutheran Church. Recently, on the occasion of the second millennium, Rome formally accepted the *Augsburg Confession*. Had an enlightened pope done so in 1530, the Church would have been spared centuries of agony.

Once again, as late as 1541, four years before the Council of Trent opened, the reformers sought reconciliation. This time the stakes were higher but nothing of biblical or even traditional substance was at issue. The reformers made four proposals: a married priesthood; communion in both forms; an affirmation of real Eucharistic presence but without the language of transubstantiation; and papal primacy without universal jurisdiction.

Rome could have accepted the first three readily. Transubstantiation was a term coined for the first time just a few centuries earlier. The Council of Trent had not yet been summoned and so transubstantiation did not have the strong conciliar endorsement it received there. Papal primacy was also ready for reform. Just a century before, the Council of Constance had called for ecumenical councils every twenty–five years, as a way of balancing that primacy.

Rome, however, gave not an inch. Soon it was too late. By 1545, a Council is convened at Trent, without Luther. He had appealed for the pope time and again to call a council and invite the Reformers. Luther died two months after Trent assembled.

MODERNISM

The medieval papacy preserved by the Council of Trent was on a collision course with the modern era. It was grieved by the Enlightenment and the scientific method, by Galileo and democracy, by the American and French Revolutions and by almost all the fundamental freedoms which define modern life.

Let us begin this reflection with Gregory XVI (1831–1846), the last pope to preside over the Papal States for his entire term of office. He was chosen after a long, fifty–day conclave because of his deep suspicions about the contemporary world.

Gregory, for example, condemned railroads and refused to allow them in the Papal States, calling them "engines from hell." He railed against street lamps fearing they would give revolutionaries an opportunity to gather and plot by night.

Gregory issued the encyclical *Mirari Vos* (1832) the year after his election. This charter for his pontificate denounced freedom of conscience as a kind of madness, freedom of the press and the separation of Church and State. The United States had written these freedoms into its Constitution four decades earlier. Gregory, furthermore, resisted the emerging Italian State, setting a pattern that would endure at the Vatican for the next hundred years.

The forces moving the Church into the modern era remained, nonetheless, powerful and unrelenting. Railroads were built around the Papal States and street lamps were lighted; constitutions were written and fundamental freedoms were guaranteed by democratic governments. Rome stopped nothing but its own progress.

The next pope, Pius IX (1846–1878), made some accommodations as his pontificate began. He freed prisoners from papal jails and seemed open to some aspects of Italian nationalism.

The crisis came when people demanded change as a right of their own rather than as a papal privilege. When a constitution was proposed for the Papal States, Pius opposed it vigorously.

Reaction was swift and violent. His prime minister, Count Rossi, was assassinated in 1848. Terrified, Pius fled in disguise to Gaeta in Southern Italy for almost a year and a half. He returned to Rome in 1850 under the protection of French troops.

He ordered the papal army to fight the Italian Risorgimento. In 1860, the army was destroyed and the Papal States seized, except for Rome where French soldiers held the city.

Pius blamed modernity for what he believed was a catastrophic defeat for the papacy. He put swiftly into place an arsenal of weapons against contemporary thought. *The Syllabus of Errors* (1864) insisted that the papacy would not be reconciled with progress, liberalism, and modern civilization. Four years later, in 1868, he excommunicated Catholics who participated in the new Italian Government. In 1870, he wrested from Vatican I his prized declaration of papal infallibility, now a defined dogma.

There were objections to the unrelenting assault. John Henry Newman refused to attend Vatican I and called supporters of Pius IX "an insolent and aggressive faction." He hoped that a future council would rescue the Church from the liabilities of Vatican I. He observed that a papacy of twenty years or more was unhealthy for both pope and Church.

Nothing, however, stopped the onward march of history. Two months after the definition of papal infallibility, the Italian army seized Rome and Pius retreated to Vatican City in a self–imposed imprisonment. The Italian Government offered Pius personal immunity, sovereignity for Vatican City State, compensation for lost territories and extra–territorial status of large numbers of universities, churches, seminaries and embassies throughout Rome. Pius would have none of it.

In such an all–out war on modernity, theologians and scholars who sought a reconciliation with the new age were brave indeed. We gain some insight into Rome's mood by the term it used to vilify them, "Modernists."

The most prominent of the Modernists was a French priest, Alfred Loisy, whose field was biblical studies. He observed that Scripture was not intended to be science or critical history. This already caused him trouble. His book, *Gospel and Church* (1903) went further and critiqued the Greek categories in which Catholic Christology is written. These categories distort the biblical image of Jesus, portraying him as a Son of God with clear Platonic insight into everything rather than as a prophet whose consciousness develops in a fully human manner.

Loisy claims, additionally, that Jesus had no intention of establishing a Church and therefore gave no explicit directions for Church structures or a papacy. These developed as the early Christians dealt with pressures imposed on them by their culture and history.

The Modernist criticism was far reaching. Nothing quite like it had been seen since the Reformation. Loisy went further and noted that Church doctrine is not unchangeable truth but an expression of how the Church experienced God and Christ at a particular point in its history.

Loisy was neither blameless nor unerring in his work. Nor was the papacy. He did, however, raise the right questions and even provided some impressive answers.

The response of Rome was swift and cruel. In 1907, Pius X (1903–1914) condemned all of Loisy's precepts, excommunicated him and other Modernists and required Catholic pastors and theology professors to take an oath against Modernism.

Vigilance committees were set up from the Vatican with informers throughout the world and a secret code for filing reports. Any charge was enough to disrupt a life; evidence and due process were disregarded. A modern-day witch hunt against learning ensued and the quality of Catholic scholarship withered.

When German armies invaded Belgium in World War I they discovered some of these coded documents and enemies' lists but assumed they had uncovered not Church reports but a spy network put in place by the allies.

The causalities of that period included Catholic integrity, Catholic justice and simple honesty. Scholars said things they did not believe to preserve their careers. Judicial proceedings in Rome were not public, appeals were not allowed, legal counsel not permitted, accusers not identified, innocence never presumed.

Rome rejected more than Loisy and the Modernists. It went at its task so insensitively that it rejected the spirit of an age. Pius X imprisoned himself and the official Church in the past as surely as Pius IX had once imprisoned himself in the Vatican.

Rome would not, of course, prevail in the long run.

The ecclesial nightmare would be over on the morning of October 11, 1962 when John XXIII would open the Second Vatican Council proclaiming that our era is a good time and that everything, including our differences, leads to the Church's growth. In the past the Church condemned people "with the greatest severity." It is time for mercy instead of harshness, a time to demonstrate the validity of Church teaching, without condemnations. "Violence inflected on others" solves nothing; love alone creates the Church and the world the Gospel intended.

In Vatican II, Luther and the Modernists would find a home for many of their ideas. It is ironic that they would be more at home in such a Council than Pius IX and Pius X. The popes who condemned these thinkers would also have condemned Vatican II had its documents been written earlier.

If Vatican I was the last medieval Council, Vatican II was the first modern Council. It brought Luther and Loisy, the Reformation and Modernism into the Catholic Church.

It took five centuries for Luther's ideas to reach the Catholic Church because a Council, Trent, had explicitly condemned his thinking. It did not require a Council to condemn Loisy because, after Vatican I, the pope was seen as a Council in his own person.

Loisy was isolated and defeated because the Pope was judged, after Vatican I, not as part of the Church but as the whole Church in himself.

By 1950, if one were to assess the Catholic Church, one would have been convinced no changes were possible and contemporary scholarship would not reach it. The list of condemned behaviors and teachings was impressive: divorce and remarriage, married priesthood, abortion of course, homosexuality, Communism and Protestantism, Orthodoxy and separation of Church and State, ecumenism and modern biblical studies, vernacular liturgy and birth control, public schools and missing Mass and meat on Friday and the many books on the Index. A Catholic in 1950 walked in a mine field in negotiating the modern world. Eighty years after the Papal States were lost and the pope was declared infallible, the papacy dominated Catholic life as never before in its history. The pope lost the Papal States but conquered the Catholic world. Vatican I triumphed and Catholics fled from modern thought, the world at large, other Christian Churches and religions as though they were incarnations of Satan. Suspicion was everywhere; doubt was nowhere. On the level of everyday life, things were less grim. Social justice healing and acts of kindness, Catholic action to make the world a better place, hospitals, schools and orphanages siphoned off Catholic energy in creative projects. But the Catholic conscience was deeply troubled, the Catholic laity thoroughly docile, the Catholic clergy fully in command, the Catholic Church a militant bastion and fortress against much of what the second millennium accomplished.

Fifty years later, in the year 2000, the Catholic world of 1950 is incredible to young people and rejected almost in its entirety by Catholics at large.

The conservative and reactionary policies of John Paul II must contend with an Ecumenical Council, Vatican II, which moved the Church in the direction of reform, and indeed, with the memory of a Pope, John XXIII, who witnessed a different style of leadership. Neither Luther nor Loisy had such a council or such a Pope.

Today the climate is different and a reformed Church is a certainty.

Vatican II called for collegiality. No one can deny that. It called for freedom of conscience. No one can deny that. It called for ecumenical and inter–religious dialogue. No one can deny that. It adopted the cry of the Reformation, "ecclesia semper reformanda," the Church must be continually reformed. No one can deny that. It called for an approach to Scripture which the Modernists favored, historically critical, exegetically rigorous. No one can deny that.

None of these attitudes or policies was in place, indeed all of them were condemned when Luther and Loisy were on the scene. Today, even John Paul II recognizes that these reforms are Catholic policy. One might interpret them narrowly but one cannot deny their validity.

For the first time in centuries we are dealing with a papacy that does not have an ecumenical council at its disposal for its reactionary agenda.

After Trent and after Loisy's excommunication, Catholics saw resistance to Luther and to Modernism as a sign of Catholic loyalty and fidelity. When the papacy did endorse modest reforms, for example, under Pius XII when the communion fast was modified and the Holy Week Liturgy renewed, these reforms came as a surprise. They were confusing and eventually accepted not because they were seen as valuable in themselves but because the Pope permitted them. Ironically, even progressive policies reinforced the conservative allegiance of Catholics to a pope who could lead them anywhere because he was Christ's Vicar. Reform was seen as the Pope's prerogative; there was no right to reform emerging from the faith of the Church at large or even in the name of the Gospel.

The Catholic response today is different. It measures the papacy by what are considered higher norms: Vatican II, Scripture, even pastoral experience. Statistics such as we see now were unimaginable during the centuries after the Reformation. Today Catholics in substantial numbers support and enact contrary positions to papal policies and teachings, even those seen by the Pope as touching on the substance of Revelation itself. Most Catholics today, certainly in this country, see the Pope as

Christ's disciple, not Christ's Vicar, as the Church's presiding bishop, not as its infallible teacher, as a sincere and perhaps holy priest, not as the Spirit's preferred spokesperson.

And so, the situation today is thoroughly different.

This papacy is the only one to have begun in the last five centuries (apart from the short tenure of John Paul I) with these "higher norms," so to speak, in place. When Catholics dissented with their behavior in the past, for example, the large number who practiced birth control before Vatican II, they accepted that they were wrong, that their behavior was sinful but that they were driven to what they did by necessity. They assumed they were sinners because the Pope told them that they were.

The deep respect Catholics maintain for the papacy in general and John Paul II in particular is premised on a papacy kept in its place, so to speak, by higher norms, a papacy Catholics can easily dissent from with impunity. Catholics will no longer give up their behavior or convictions only because the Pope orders them to do so.

All this is not seen by Catholics at large as defiance or as sin, not even as an unwarranted way of being a Catholic. It is, in its own way, an oblique consultation of the laity when no formal consultation is available. It is collegiality by default when no meaningful collegiality is in place. It is less self–indulgence or cafeteria Catholicism than it is conscience Catholicism asserting, as John Henry Newman noted, the priority of conscience to the Pope. In its own way, it is a quiet, relentless, irreversible way of going about reform. If the reform is not official it will continue nonetheless, as water does, seeking its own level no matter how it is obstructed.

Were the papacy able to enforce its decision by law as it did in the Middle Ages so that artificial birth control and abortion and homosexual relationships and marriage after divorce and optional celibacy were interdicted by law and even punished by the State, Catholics would rebel. Indeed the State protects all Catholics who choose these alternatives from Church abuse. The fact that Catholics can go their own way has preserved the papacy. The papacy prevails today because it is singularly impotent. It reaches especially those it carefully selects as loyalists and those already embittered by modernity. This impotence allows the Pope to be celebrated as a symbol of ideals. Pius IX was never more celebrated than when he was rendered impotent by the loss of the Papal States. John Paul II has lost the Papal States, so to speak, of Catholic conscience and conviction. He is celebrated for what he chooses not to be, a symbol rather than a teacher, a fallible but beloved figure rather than an infallible guide for Catholic identity.

Vatican II liberated Catholics more deeply than most realize. It was not only the heady issues of liturgical reform, collegiality, conscience, religious liberty, ecumenism, biblical studies and modernity which made the difference but something more profound.

Catholics discovered new norms, without always being fully cognizant, to guide their future lives. Scripture, personal experience, and the unwritten spirit of Vatican II would now be alternatives to papal authoritarianism.

The Church now became a place for all God's People and not only an enshrined hierarchical presence. The Church would still be a resource for Catholics at large, at times a deeply moving resource, indeed a home which they affirmed with affection. It would never again become for them, however, the Pope's home, one in which patriarchal dominion required obedience of all the inhabitants, a dominion in which dissent was punished and in which even those being punished believed they deserved the punishment. Such a partiarchial home, I suggest, is still, it pains me to obverse, the model and the ecclesiology of John Paul II. It has no chance of prevailing.

It took a century once to build a Temple in Jerusalem. That Temple was destroyed in four years by the Roman armies. A century after the definition of papal infallibility, the structure built on it was effectively destroyed in fours years by Vatican II. If God no longer dwells in a Temple, then God must be found in God's People. A temple is never a home; people at large, however, know how to build communities and homes. We were once strangers in the Temple of the Church we once loved. We have become, as of late, a family in the home of our own lives.

CONCLUSION

Catholic reformers curiously are driven by the ideals and visions of a future Church and become easily discouraged when they must settle for the present Church. It is, furthermore, difficult for Catholic reformers to be responsive to the lessons of history since they look back less willingly than conservatives do. Yet it is the very patterns of the past and the very dynamics of the present Church which can reinforce their hope.

There are two fears Catholic reformers experience. One of these is the fear that the restorationist agenda will prevail, that the cause will be lost, that the guiding spirit of a future church will be Pius IX and not John XXIII.

There is no possibility, as I see it, that the cause will be lost. Looking at the past one can understand that the Reformation succeeded far more than Luther imagined and even in areas where he did not envision reform. The substance of the Reformation is now Catholic doctrine and Catholic conviction.

And Modernism abides at the heart of Catholic identity today. Even a reactionary such as John Paul II would not affirm that Moses composed the Torah and that Genesis is scientifically accurate in contemporary terms. A predecessor of John Paul II, however, censured and excommunicated Alfred Loisy for these very declarations. In the vast majority of Catholic universities around the world it is taught that Jesus did not explicitly found a Church and, indeed, that history played a decisive role in the development of Church structure and papal office. Indeed ecumenical dialogue today takes all this for granted.

Contemporary Catholic Christology has a place for the developing consciousness of Jesus. Vatican II endorsed modernity and stated that the Church could learn from it.

Loisy and the Modernists did not imagine that a Council and a Pope and the informed Catholic community at large would one day accept all this.

And so the cause cannot be lost because only a Pope opposes it. The Council and the People of God are more than any Pope. Even reactionaries would understand this.

There is a second fear among Catholic reformers, a melancholy that they will not live to see their dreams realized. There is a sadness that we shall not see what we worked so hard, so whole–heartedly, so hopefully, to build. There is a distress that we shall die on the borders of the Promised Land as did Moses who looked longingly on the Land he could not enter, the goal of all his dreams. There is a sorrow that we shall die as Martin Luther King did surveying from the mountain top of his hopes the possibilities he would not experience.

We might remind ourselves that the Promised Land was sweeter to Moses from a distance and that the land of milk and honey, once inhabited, became also a land of blood and tears. And should we not note that Martin Luther King would hardly find present day America a Promised Land.

We might add a further thought. Is it not possible that we are already in the Promised Land and do not know it? Odysseus in Homer's *Odyssey*, is home, in the land of his dreams, long before he realizes where he is.

How, some might object, can we call this the Promised Land when we hurt so much, when we have a Pope who seems at times more Pharaoh than Shepherd?

But are we not already in the Promised Land when we have been liberated in our hearts, when the task master is no longer the norm, when enough of the desert has been passed for us to know there will be no turning back, when the future is already here, not in its fullness, but in the first Springtime of its promise?

Clearly we are in the Promised Land, at last on its borders, when we feel free to do all that was unfairly denied us before we arrived.

If we hold to the course set by the Second Vatican Council in the face of contrary winds pushing us back to the desert of our distress, to the Egypt of our former bondage, if we press on, then we are truly free and are, in a sense, already home. For we no longer require the task master for our security and for our identity. And we are no longer beguiled by the many collaborators, and co–conspirators, once former friends, who serve the oppressor. We learn to forgive this and to press on, with all humility and without rancor, because we are no longer defined by all that was but abide, rather, in a new place, a safe place, a promised homeland.

We were sent on this mission not by our own choice but by a Council we did not choose and a Pope we did not expect and a Spirit that led us to know we were not home where we once were.

We may yet be denied the formal recognition by the Church of the reforms we sought. But they are alive in our hearts, purified in the crucible of the long struggle and the long journey.

If the reforms had come more quickly and more easily they would have shaped our faith and fidelity less deeply. And we would have been grateful to an institutional Church for giving us so readily reforms that were never truly ours, for which we had not suffered.

There would have been losses either way. By not having much sooner the Church we labored to build, we endured isolation and exhaustion, compelled to act in a contrary way when this was not our nature, embarrassed by an institutional Church we loved.

But had the Church of Vatican II come about more quickly, there still would have been disappointments and reverses, tears and labor, since no Church is ideal.

Married priests might have been granted canonical ministry in a Church which remained angry at their choice. Women may have been ordained into a Church system which would yet exclude them. Divorced Catholics might become fully part of the Church's life but still feel the sting of self–righteousness from unhappily married Catholics. Even a Church with a less rigid sexual ethic could not free us from the complications of sorting out our own sexual options in the isolation of our own conscience.

I do not wish to give the impression that the delayed reform has not been tragic. Nor do I underestimate the pain and suffering it has caused. Nor do I choose to be foolishly patient and understanding in the face of so much hard–heartedness and cruelty, inflicted often by leaders ever eager for their own careers.

In any case, this is how it went.

It was glorious to have been part of such an era in human and Church history. It is, after all, life itself which breaks our hearts and mends them, not a particular moment in history. Suffering is never missed. Nor is joy. Nor is grace.

At any point in which we enter the river of life we may find that the currents are different but some of them will always be contrary. It is not possible to find an ideal place to enter the river. In any case, the river runs to the same sea. It is there that we find God who teaches us to look back on the journey with joy. When one arrives, if the passage was more difficult for one of us than the other, for such a person the sea is more splendid.

I remember once as a young professor in the seminary, thirty two years of age, swimming alone before breakfast on a July morning in a remote area of the Seminary property. I loved the stillness, the contemplative silence, the isolation. I did not realize the danger until I was seized with an inability to swim and began to drown. It was useless to cry for help. I remember deciding that I would cease trying to reach the shore in a moment and allow myself to drown since I was exhausted by my wild effort to reach safety.

I wondered why it was necessary for me to die so young and so soon, before I had a chance to do all the glorious things I thought possible. And I grieved at the grief my parents and sister would suffer.

Would all my dreams die with me, I remember asking as I struggled and gasped and went down. Would I find God in the depths to which I was falling?

Suddenly I felt a surge of energy and started to move toward shore. I prayed in wild mantras that the energy would not leave me before the shore. When I finally arrived and felt the earth, I laughed and wept and remained a long time silent. Eventually I felt strong enough to stand and walked back to my room

How much I would have lost had the swim that morning gone easily!

4

THE CONVERSIONS OF
THOMAS MERTON

John Henry Newman once observed that a faith which is ready to believe whatever it is told is a faith of no substance. Faith and grace are more demanding and more serious than that.

On the occasion of Thomas Merton's sixtieth anniversary of baptism (November 16, 1938) and in this very church of Corpus Christi where his baptism was celebrated, we might explore our connection with that event and with his life. His struggle and achievement may provide insight into our own lives and journeys.

I would like to comment on what I see as the eight conversion experiences of Thomas Merton.

SPIRITUALITY

Not long after his father's death, Merton, an orphan and in his late teens, travels to Rome. He is searching for meaning and stability after the trauma of losing both parents. He has been victimized in ways he finds confusing by his mother's coldness and his father's indifferent parenting.

One night, in his room, he believes he senses his father's presence. It seems to summon him from a life of secularism and self–indulgence to a life of deeper meanings and mystical connections.

The experience is shattering. Writing about it years later, he can still feel how "vivid" and "real" it was, how intense and urgent was the summons to a change of heart and spirit.

He prays and weeps and reaches out for all that he has lost and for all he yearns to gain.

A conversion need not be complete for it to be permanent. Merton did not live an exemplary life after this but he was substantially changed by it.

The origins of his baptism, some five years later, can be traced to this experience. It is instructive to note that his initial call to God happens without much reference to the institutional Church and its sacramental system. His later conversions, in the last decade of his life, will repeat this pattern.

BAPTISM

During the next five years, Merton experiences further dislocation. He loses the support of those, like Dr. Thomas Bennett, who had become his guardian. He drifts into alcoholism and sexual excess. He leaves his studies in Cambridge University fleeing to the United States in a rather dishonorable effort to avoid a paternity suit. There are no abiding friendships and not much personal responsibility and maturity. The conversion to spirituality seems to have been an aberration, an illusion, one more step in a journey of disenchantment and betrayal.

In February of 1935, Merton enrolls in Columbia University and meets regularly with one of its great professors, Mark Van Doren. He finds a circle of friends and associates (Lax, Giroux, Rice, Freedgood, Rhinehart) who become life–long companions and colleagues. The spiritual search goes beyond a mystical experience in isolation to include friendship, human sharing and community. He finds hope in a Church ready to accept him since there is no hope when he is left to his own devices. Catholicism rescues him from pessimism and wandering.

There are other deaths in the family, the beginning of a career in writing, and encounters with Hindu and Christian authors. The texture of his life deepens and he feels called to spirituality again, but this time in a communal and traditional context. He turns to Catholicism and finds at Corpus Christi a faith life which nurtures him.

He describes in his autobiography, *Seven Storey Mountain*, the anxiety and exigency which lead him to ask for baptism:

"What are you waiting for?"

"Why do you still hesitate?"

"It's absurd."

"Suddenly, I could bear it no longer. I put down the book, and got into my raincoat and...went out into the street...I had nine blocks to walk."

Merton goes to Corpus Christi and informs Rev. George Ford: "I want to become a Catholic."

Baptism for him means entering the Catholic Church, canceling out "twenty three black years of sin," ending his "slavery to death," bringing him, if not to Paradise, to at least the "seven–circled mountain of Purgatory."

MONASTICISM

Three years after his baptism, Merton enters the Abbey of Gethsemani as a monk. The three years have led him into doctoral work in literature and into teaching English at St. Bonaventure College in New York. He writes unpublished novels, begins to work at Friendship House in Harlem and experiences the painful rejection of his application to become a Franciscan.

The desire in Merton's heart is to become a priest. The spirituality conversion led to baptism. The baptismal conversion leads to monasticism. The connections are not anticipated but they fit.

In Havana, Cuba, Merton receives a positive answer to his tormented questions about whether he would be acceptable to God as a monk or a priest. He is struck at a Sunday liturgy by an experience as intense as the encounter with his deceased father which started it all a short seven years ago. This time it is "God's presence" and "heaven...right here in front of me" which he experiences. He is left with "a breathless joy and a clean peace and happiness" that he never forgot. He is renewed with confidence in his calling and with a sense that he is on the right road. He returns to the United States a changed man. In December of 1941, he sends most of his clothes to Friendship House for the poor, burns the novels he has written, and boards an evening train for the journey to Kentucky and Gethsemani where he will remain for the next twenty seven years of his life.

This is a long–delayed and perilous conversion. It is a turning to the world and its values. It is the indispensable means to the remaining conversions of Merton's life. One might date this conversion to the late 1950's, a decade and a half or so after his entrance into Gethsemani. He is a celebrated writer, the author of *Seven Storey Mountain*, a spiritual master, a priest and a poet.

Merton had been so bruised and betrayed by the secular world that, initially, he wanted no part of it. Indeed, he wanted the whole world to cease being the world and to become a monastery. He saw the world as an unsafe zone, a hostile environment where goodness happened against the odds.

The monastic life prepared Merton, paradoxically, to accept the world by taking him from it and by allowing him to see that his problems were not caused by the world but by his own heart.

There is a pattern in Merton's life. Before major decisions, he undergoes a profound mystical experience which assures him that he is not wrong and that God is with him. Thus, he turns to the spiritual life when he encounters a vision of his deceased father; he becomes a monk after a sense of God's presence at a liturgy in Havana; he accepts his calling to be engaged with the world and to struggle for social justice after an experience in Louisville. On a crowded street corner he is thrown into waves of emotional turmoil and tranquillity as he sees the crowds of people around him as good and valuable in their own humanity, in their own right, without reference to Church or monastery. In *Conjectures of a Guilty Bystander*, he describes the moment in which he cries out in his own soul: "Thank God. Thank God that I am like other men." He sees separation from the world as an illusion and is convinced that people are filled with light, "shining like the sun."

Merton is too discriminating a thinker to endorse everything human as graced. He comes to see, however, late in his monastic life, that being human is a sacramental experience and that people can be validated in their own humanity if they do not distort it. It is not baptism or Church or monastery which is the source of human goodness but something much deeper. It is the fact that we are made in God's image. This justifies even when we are not part of the Church and even if we are against some of its policies.

There is peril, of course, in basing decisions on subjective, non–rational, mystical experiences. How can one be responsible if one builds a life on an encounter with a deceased parent, an exuberant moment in a liturgy, an emotional reaction on a crowded street corner?

The peril is lessened if these experiences are balanced by subsequent, critical thinking and validated in community life. Merton, after all, cannot become a monk without the review of others. He does not become a prophet for social justice without reference to the bracing realism of Scripture and Church Tradition.

This conversion to the world is the most radical of Merton's conversions and the least expected. Conversions to spirituality, baptism and monastery are more easily explained in conventional categories. The conversion to the world, however, is less customary. Such a conversion may appear to reverse the previous conversions and to be self–indulgent. Merton had once been in the world without the benefit of conversion and he had found chaos and darkness. Ironically, the conversion to the world makes even more imperative his clinging to spirituality, baptism, and monastery.

PEOPLE OF GOD

While all this is going on, the Catholic Church at large is undergoing a conversion we call the Second Vatican Council. The Council puts Merton's previous conversions in a different context. There is a new interpretation of spirituality, bringing into play the values of conscience, the centrality of Scripture and the notion that there is a universal call to holiness that goes far beyond formal religious communities. Baptism is presented as a summons to a discipleship of equals and to a mystery which is more fundamental than the Church's hierarchical and clerical structures. Indeed, even the concept of monasticism is changed as the Council calls upon religious communities to re–think their mission, their way of life, their charter and their rules. The world itself is celebrated in a major document on the Church in the modern world.

If Merton had been led in these directions by intuition, mystical yearnings and his own experience, he suddenly finds all this endorsed by his Church on the highest level of its teaching in an Ecumenical Council.

Merton proclaims a new spirituality, one less obediential and pious, less traditional and ecclesiastical. He addresses with favor humanists who do not believe in God and believers who believe differently from the way Christians do. He feels called not only by the Church but by the civil rights movement, not only by the hierarchy endorsing just wars but by prophets calling for non–violence, not only by the Vatican Council but also by the Vietnam protest.

Merton sees the Church as God's People and sees all people as God's family, not in some abstract and rhetorical fashion but as a living, concrete reality.

Merton becomes more like that Christ who was not a temple priest and who was not endorsed by the official religion of his own time. He becomes more like that Jesus whose baptism began his ministry without fully defining and institutionalizing it.

Jesus is not a Jewish monk, although such existed in the Dead Sea communities of his own day. He is a monk in the world, so to speak, who found his consecration in healing others, indeed in healing the very religion of Judaism. Jesus is a monk in the world who prays in the mountains rather than in a monastery and who defines his ministry in his conscience and in the deeper traditions of Jewish spirituality.

For Merton, contemplation was for everyone and mysticism was a universal calling. No one was excluded from the People of God, even those who formally rejected paths to God approved by the Church.

RELIGIONS OF THE HUMAN FAMILY

The Vatican II conversion which enables Merton to be committed to the Church in a radically new way leads to the even more rarefied conversion of discovering holiness and grace and God in the other religions of the human family. Indeed, not only are these values present there but they are sometimes more abundantly there. Christianity, therefore, does not teach the other religions without learning from them. Christianity is not a religious system with complete and comprehensive insight into God and holiness but a partner with other religions in affirming a God who is beyond all of them.

We are now some thirty years after Merton's baptism and he is in a place he could not have foreseen. In 1938, Merton would have rejected vehemently the central affirmations of his life in 1968.

Merton does not endorse the other religions without controversy. He loses readers and gains critics, forfeits friends and attracts censors.

Nonetheless, he explores the outer limits of what the incarnation entails. The incarnation tells us that God became comprehensively human, not exclusively Jewish. Merton finds it difficult to exclude anything human from God's incarnational embrace, especially the world religions by which people find and celebrate the God they have experienced.

Once again, Merton finds certitude through a mystical experience. Standing before statues of Buddha in a journey to Asia to pray with contemplatives from other religions, Merton cries out, in a moment of revelation, that he has discovered, "All I was obscurely looking for..." He writes in his journal just days before his death that he has finally "got beyond the shadow and disguise" of life. It is Buddhism which helps him reach this plateau.

FEMININE

This is the most formidable of all the conversions to assess, perhaps because there is something so personally unique and baffling about it.

Merton falls romantically in love with a young nurse in 1966, twenty five years into his monastic life and two years before his death.

How does one account for a relationship that seems so disruptive coming as it does late in Merton's life and challenging the authenticity of many of the previous conversions?

There are those who see this as the undoing of the conversion to spirituality and as a return to self–indulgence and immaturity. The critics should not be dismissed summarily.

The love relationship raises the right questions for us even if we may not approve of it. God is the author of romantic love and sexuality and yet many people are deeply suspicious of both when they do not occur in categories approved by Church teaching. It is easier for many to allow Merton to challenge Church doctrine or policy in other areas than these.

I believe that Merton's experience of romantic love has its roots in two issues. One of these is a conversion to feminine values in his personal and religious life. Merton turns more and more frequently to mysticism, to pacifism, to Buddhism, to harmony and tranquillity. To this, one must add an affection, erotic and spiritual all at once, for a nurse named Margaret. The more feminine Catholicism Merton accepts is less militant and aggressive, less exclusive and judgmental. It has fewer boundaries. It is heavily invested in collegiality and dialogue, in relationships and personalism. There is danger in this new approach but the former ways of proceeding were not without problems.

The second of these two issues is the resolution of the erotic and the spiritual. Merton moved in his earlier life toward the erotic and away from the spiritual. There may have been elements of rage and desperation in this. The rage may have derived from his anger with his inadequate parents and also from their early deaths; the desperation may have been an effort to achieve an intimacy he never knew by substituting eroticism for relationship.

There are genuine dimensions of both eroticism and spirituality but Merton cannot find the balance in his early life. He begins to identify all eroticism as darkness as he feels called to holiness. He buries eroticism in a piety which seeks to eliminate not only the excesses to which eroticism can lead but also its values and its graces. He represses rather than resolves his conflicts.

He tells us in *Seven Storey Mountain* that he resisted "any kind of possessive attention on the part of any other human being" and that he had a "profound instinct to keep clean, to keep free." Such an attitude can easily become evasion and escape. Rage and desperation are the other side of fear. Fear keeps one running away. In *Sign of Jonas* Merton is even more blunt. He tells us he "cannot possess created things" or even "touch them." Merton renounces his sexuality in order to become spiritual because he knew how powerful and destructive his sexual instincts were.

Some of this seems to have been going on during his preparation for baptism in 1938. He tells us in his autobiography that he was reading widely the poetry of Richard Crashaw (1613–1649). Crashaw's poetry is charged with sexual and spiritual energy. I suspect that Merton finds in Crashaw a healthy resolution of the tension he himself was not handling well. Crashaw's poem on Teresa of Avila, "The Flaming Heart," is one of the most erotic and mystical poems I have ever read. Does Merton see here his own dilemma and his own incapacity to settle it effectively?

In any case, the unfinished agenda with eroticism returns when he falls in love with Margaret. This is the first time in his life a human and erotic relationship is worthy of poetry, a lot of poetry, some of it the best he ever wrote. I know of no other poems of Merton to someone he loved romantically during the twenty six years before he became a monk. With Margaret, the erotic has become a love experience and a spiritual one.

In an earlier journal, *Vow of Conversation*, in a passage on the eve of his fiftieth birthday, about a year before he met Margaret, he writes with disappointment about how badly his relationships with women and sexual experience had gone and of how much he yearned for the roads he had not traveled.

Merton finds with Margaret a woman he loved more completely than any other woman he had known before her. The erotic and mystical are not polar opposites in the world Merton discovers with her.

The Margaret experience may be viewed in different ways. I do not pretend to have the conclusive answer. Margaret may have been a mistake, a lapse, something which should not have happened, a moment of weakness, a source of regret and even shame. I am suggesting, however, that Margaret was an experience of conversion, a call to a deeper holiness, a reconciliation of opposites in his spiritual life.

The key question posed by Margaret is how important relationships are in the spiritual journey. Catholic spirituality has sometimes judged them as less worthy. Indeed, if they are erotic, they are often seen as corrupting. The platonic and celibate relationship is proposed as the ideal for holiness. There were times in its history when the Catholic Church counseled celibate marriages as the way to perfection for Christians who were not monks.

Merton writes compelling poetry, as we have said, about Margaret and himself. It is not poetry which rejects the erotic as evil, even though he may have felt this in his early religious life and, perhaps, until he met her. He once feared physical contact as a danger to spiritual development. Now, however, he is in a different place. Margaret is a danger but also a grace. In this case, the grace cannot be given without the danger. Merton finds in Margaret something beautiful, valuable, irreplaceable. He finds himself and God in a new way through this experience. There is less terror and greater peace and a more expansive openness to all that

is human. There are moments of folly, of course, but all folly is not foolish.

I asked Abbot Flavian Burns, Merton's confessor, about Margaret
and the mystical life of Merton. He was convinced that Merton was the
greatest mystic he had ever encountered. The Margaret experience did
not change his evaluation.

Richard Crashaw, the poet Merton read as he prepared for baptism,
wrote of Teresa of Avila in sexual and mystical language. Merton, at the
end of his life, uses the same language in his poetry about Margaret. The
end, at times, can be so much like the beginning.

I believe Margaret represented a conversion for Merton. A conversion need not be perfect or complete for it to be right and good. A conversion is not just an event; it is also a process. The process lingers long
after the event has passed. It may go on as a love experience even when
the other person has left the scene. Indeed the influence of someone we
love can be greater in that person's absence. Margaret may have taught
Merton to trust his mysticism more than his monasticism, his conscience more than convention, his intrinsic responsibility more than the
approved rules. She led him beyond the continence and abstinence of
his life to a world of passion which had its own authenticity.

DEATH

Death could not be proud in the ending of Merton's life. It is not
death which prevails but the conversion of Merton through and beyond
it into a symbol where opposites converge, where East meets West (he
dies in Asia), where Buddhism encounters Christianity (he dies at a conference of contemplatives from both traditions), where the world and
monasticism reach harmony (the talk he delivers on the day of his death
deals with Marxism as monasticism).

Had Merton lived longer he might have become less. It is difficult to
imagine how he might have become more. Death has a way of finishing
the unfinished business of our lives, of endowing the lives it terminates
with more life than they may have achieved on their own. Death con-
verts Merton into a universal symbol of extraordinary proportions.

CONCLUSION

It was a hero's journey, this life of Merton, undertaken with enormous risk and completed successfully not only for himself but for all of us. We are different, better, more confident because of his life.

On November 16, 1938, the journey began with an earnestness it never lost. It took surprising directions and scaled unanticipated heights.

On the day he was baptized in this church he could still recall that night in Rome when he sensed his father's presence. The monastery was a faint hope in his mind. He could not then, however, embrace the world which bruised him so much and which he abused. The Church he was baptized into was not a Church for all God's People as he would later understand it. Neither Buddha nor women in general nor Margaret in particular could be seen on the distant horizon of his future.

He expected to die a Catholic, perhaps a monk. That was believable in 1938. Instead he died with the world at his side and all God's People mourning the loss of a prophet and spiritual guide who made life bearable and hopeful. He died after having learned to find Christ in Buddha and after he had fallen in love with a woman he could never forget, a woman whose heart was shattered by the news of his death.

Had the journey gone foreword conventionally we would have lost so much, he would have grown so little.

In 1938, Merton became a son of the Church, so to speak. God made him after this a monk, a prophet to the world, a Church reformer, a Christian Buddhist and a lover of Margaret. If any of these steps were left out, Merton's life would have been incomplete. Because he took all these steps after his baptism, he became not only a son of the Church but a brother to all of us.

5

A NEW MILLENNIUM FOR MARRIED PRIESTS

Jan Kerkhofs, perhaps Europe's leading religious sociologist, is a professor emeritus of the University of Louvain, a Jesuit, and a writer of clarity and distinction.

Kerkhofs is a Belgian. He addressed the first Congress of the International Federation of Married Catholic Priests in Rome in 1987. It was he who told us that almost half of Catholic parishes worldwide had no present pastor and that lay leaders serving in the absence of a priest had very different ideas about a married priesthood, the ordination of women, and sexual ethics.

As we gathered for the semi–annual meeting of the Executive Committee of the International Federation, I inquired about Kerkhofs. I was given an interview from "The Standard" (30 September 1999), a Belgian paper.

In that article, Kerkhofs observed that the five most urgent questions facing the Church were:

Credibility (the Church for most modern people is not where they seek their values and meaning; this is true for Catholics as well as people at large)

Collegiality
(the structures of authority are in crisis)

Ministry
(Kerkhofs gave as one example of the pastoral shortage,
a 70 year old priest responsible for ten parishes)

Sexual Morality
(there is an abyss between the teaching of the hierarchy
and the convictions of the people at large)
Ecumenism
(this is a universal hope and a contemporary disappointment)

Kerkhofs noted that reactionary forces were in place from the 1971 Synod of Bishops. That Synod turned down a married priesthood by twenty votes (187–207). Forty bishops had been appointed by the Pope and the Curia. Had the Synod been represented by bishops in pastoral service and by the delegates of national hierarchies, the ordination of married men would have begun in 1971. The ambiguity of Paul VI strengthened the reactionary forces, stung and angry by the widespread rejection of *Humanae Vitae* (the 1968 encyclical prohibiting all means of artificial contraception, in all cases).

A target of reactionary bishops was the International Synod, set up by Vatican II as a balancing voice to the Curia and as a means for bishops in pastoral service to influence Rome and the papacy. These Synods were described as "sterile" by the late Cardinal Joseph Bernardin after they had been altered by John Paul II. Similar comments were made by Cardinal Danneels of Belgium, and by Archbishop John Quinn, former President of the United States Catholic Bishops.

Kerkhofs criticized the Pope for making the Synod an instrument of Vatican policy rather than a collegial structure of the world–wide Church. The result has been what Kerkhofs calls a "sociological schism" between the "Holy See and a world moving into its future." As the schism gains energy and the Vatican feels powerless to control it, the papacy relies on authority to settle what only consensus can achieve. "If the Church needs infallibility to answer a question, it has nothing to say." The prophetic leadership this Church requires is not a counter–cultural, lonely voice seeking to clarify everything but a call for people to search for answers together in communities of conscience and concern.

The secularization of the moment is not necessarily an evil. It has raised old questions with a new urgency. Who is God? Why is Christ important? Is there life after death, for Jesus and for us? Secularization makes good spirituality a priority. In the final analysis, spirituality preserves us in truth and in life far more effectively than all other alternatives.

For the first seven years of its existence, the International Federation held its Executive Committee Meetings in Paris (1986–1993). For the next seven years it moved its meetings to different cities of Europe in an effort to meet with local priest groups, to give interviews in the media and to worship with concerned reformed Catholics on the European continent. These dialogues enriched the Federation and made it possible for local groups to feel connected to the Federation. We met in Austria (Vienna), Belgium (Brussels), England (London), Germany (Mainz), France (Marseilles), Ireland (Dublin), Italy (Rome; Livorno), Netherlands (Amsterdam), and Spain (Madrid). During these years we convened two Congresses outside Europe (Brasilia, Brazil, 1996 and Atlanta, GA, United States of America, 1999). We had meaningful dialogues in these visits with Cardinal Schonborn of Austria, Cardinal Hume of England, the Bishops of Ireland and the Vice President of the Italian Bishops Conference.

The present meeting (March 30–April 2, 2000) marked a return to Brussels. We chose Brussels for a number of reasons. The first of these was a desire to meet with the local Belgian groups (Hors les Murs, French–speaking, and Inspraak, Flemish–speaking). A further reason was to acquaint ourselves with the culture and law of Belgium since the Federation will seek incorporation under Belgian and European Union law and will also file for Non–Governmental Organization (NGO) status with the United Nations through Brussels. United Nations recognition will give us international status, legal stability and recognition, access to grants and funding, and use of United Nations buildings and facilities for our work.

Some of our work was internal and complex. Working in a number of languages (English, French, Italian on occasion, Spanish) we began a close scrutiny of our Statutes on the basis of Belgian law and United Nations requirements. This work will require attention at the next two meetings of the Executive Committee before it is complete.

Delegates to the Executive Committee included Paul Bourgeois (Belgium), Claude Bertin (France), Heinz Vogels (Germany, delegate by invitation), Mauro del Nevo (Italy), Lambert Van Gelder (Netherlands), Aitor Orube and Julio Pinillos (Spain) and Anthony Padovano (U.S.A.).

Of more immediate interest were the initiatives we made to meet in Madrid in 2002 at a special Conference sponsored by the International Movement: We Are Church (IMWAC) and the International Federation of Married Catholic Priests (IFMCP). Various other international reform groups, yet to be determined, will co–sponsor the event. Elfriede Harth of IMWAC met with us through one morning and afternoon. This Conference will serve as a millennial celebration seeking to give common voice to the many reform organizations created in the 35 years since the close of Vatican II.

The next Congress of the International Federation will take place in 2005, quite possibly in Rome. Thus, after an absence from Europe since 1993 (Madrid), the Federation will meet again in Europe in 2002 (Madrid) and 2005 (Rome).

The Italian representative (Mauro del Nevo) has made a formal proposal for a ritual of reconciliation and solidarity between married priests and the official Church. We are awaiting a reply from the Bishops Conference of Italy for a meeting in Rome to celebrate this Event in the present calendar year. We are asking for this meeting in the light of the Jubilee spirit of the millennium.

The remainder of the Committee agenda concerned plans for future issues of *Ministerium Novum*, our superlative publication; connections with emerging international reform associations (e.g., European Network; Woman's Ordination World–Wide; Catholics for the Right to Decide); and a review of correspondence and requests from around the world (Austria, India, Indonesia, Pakistan, Poland). A Polish married priest, Roman Kotlinski, author of a best seller in Poland (100,000 copies) *The Church: a Clerical Bastian*, wrote to us about his desire to connect with married priests world–wide.

The International Federation has now completed fourteen years of work, some 30 Executive Committee meetings, and five international Congresses (Rome, Netherlands, Spain, Brazil, U.S.A.). We have had formal dialogues with Cardinals and Bishops throughout Europe and published documents on canon law and ministry, bishops and their call for reform of ministry, final declarations of international congresses, and years of *Ministerium Novum*. We have kept up a rigorous correspondence with the Vatican and given interviews in the Americas, Asia and Europe. We have gathered national groups together, inspired their newsletters, and supported them with a sense of solidarity. Bert Peeters, our first President, has written a history of the Federation; our Archives have been accepted by the University of Louvain (Belgium), the University of Koblenz (Germany) and the University of Nijmegen (Netherlands pending). Before the Federation came into existence, there were two synods on international assemblies of married priests, both in Italy (Chiusi in 1983 and Ariccia, near Rome, in 1985).

It has been a journey of grace and a pilgrimage of peace. As a new millennium begins, we have every reason to look back with humility and gratitude and forward with hope and commitment.

6

PARLIAMENT OF
WORLD RELIGIONS

CAPE TOWN, SOUTH AFRICA
DECEMBER 1 – 8, 1999

Unity is the sign of our times. The twentieth century has raised our spirits and broken our hearts. Through the agony and the ecstasy, the light of unity has burned ever more brightly. One might place the Parliament of World Religions in this context.

We have witnessed so much unity. The nineteenth century never imagined a universal nation like the United States is today or a World Council of Churches, the United Nations or a Universal Declaration of Human Rights, Vatican II or the European Union, the globalization of markets or instantaneous communication. A Parliament of World Religions emerges from such a dynamic.

Religions are not only about religion but also about politics. Every politician knows this. Religions are not only protective of human life but also, tragically, its destroyer. Every historian knows this. Religions not only enable us to order our lives but also divide us into hostile camps. Every sociologist knows this.

Nonetheless, the world has poured massive energy into religious institutions over the millennia. A gathering of all the religions of the world has the potential of being more important than any other human assembly. When religions meet today, they speak about God, of course, and of meaning, but also about world debt, ecology, population, nuclear disarmament, human rights and education.

We were meeting in South Africa and the ambiguity of religion was seen here with especial force. In 1948, apartheid was implemented in South Africa; in the same year the World Council of Churches was created. Both used religious rhetoric to justify themselves.

Hans Kung, a major voice in the Parliament, said it well. There can be no peace among nations without peace among the religions and no peace among the religions without dialogue. A Parliament of World Religions is a singular human achievement.

COMPARISONS AND GOALS

The first Parliament of World Religions met during the Columbian Exposition from September 11 – 28, 1893 at what is now the Art Institute of Chicago. Some 7,000 people attended, including Frederick Douglas. Buddhists, Christians, Confucionists and Hindus were present but invitations did not go out to Muslims, Native Americans or Sikhs. This first Parliament was significant in its very occurrence. Its greatest accomplishment was its very act of existence.

A century later, in 1993, the Parliament met again, in Chicago, at the Palmer House Hotel (August 28 – September 5). About 8,000 delegates attended. There were three significant changes in this Parliament from its predecessor. The first of these was its inclusivity; no religious group was excluded. A second feature of this Parliament was the fact that a gathering of world religions did not seem as exotic, singular, or isolated as it did in 1893. There was a world experience now able to see such an assembly as fitting and, indeed, to consider it as a means to achieve harmony among essentially isolated religious systems. The third distinctive feature was the adoption of a "Declaration Toward a Global Ethic" on September 4, 1993. For the first time, representatives of all the religions agreed on principles for a global ethic and committed themselves to non–violence, economic justice, tolerance and gender equity. The architect of the Declaration was Dr. Hans Kung of Germany, a Christian theologian.

The first Parliament demonstrated that the world religions could gather in mutual respect and dialogue. The second Parliament proved that religious traditions could achieve ethical consensus and issue a common document.

The third Parliament brought about new developments. The first of these was the agreement that such an assembly should convene at regular intervals, perhaps every five years. A second development focused on social justice issues rather than on teachings or ethics. The Parliament produced an "Earth Charter," whose operative working principle was balance between human life and the planet. Peace is presented as the result of a new relationship with the earth and of respect for the interdependency of all beings and their intrinsic worth. Peace is defined as "wholeness created by balanced and harmonious relationships with oneself, other persons, other cultures, other life."

The "Earth Charter" observes that "human development is primarily about being more, not having more." It calls for "reverence for the mystery of being, gratitude for the gift of life and humility regarding the human place in nature."

A third feature of the present Parliament was its meeting outside the United States for the first time. The Parliament is an American idea but the African location for this Parliament underscored the global acceptance of this enterprise. The United States has all the religions of the world living in its borders but the world of religion needs a home in more than one country.

Cape Town, South Africa, was selected for a number of reasons. It is the place where three continents meet, where the Atlantic and Indian Oceans converge with Africa, Asia, and Europe

Cape Town is the city where one of the great icons of the twentieth century, Nelson Mandela, endured decades of imprisonment and emerged with a message of forgiveness, non–violence, and racial harmony. Mandela paid tribute to the Parliament by changing his itinerary and postponing a trip to the United States so that he could address us.

Three goals of the Parliament were stated in its opening session:

▶ The Parliament is about harmony, not unity
▶ It is about convergence of purpose, not consensus
▶ It seeks creative engagement, not structure

Religions tend now to recognize the right of alternative religious systems to exist and the responsibility to dialogue with one another. Religious diversity is a source of celebration rather than a problem to be solved. The Parliament celebrated with a striking collage of music and song, ritual and dance, attire and prayer.

In the midst of the color and drama, there was a unifying conviction that religions are permanent human institutions and that they, collectively, have an enormous potential to change the world for the better. There was a reluctance to define what religion is exactly but a sense that the transcendent, however named or encountered, grounds our awareness of the sacred.

The Parliament is remarkable because it does not exist by the design of the world's religious leaders but comes into being by the force of the spirit of the age.

THE THIRD PARLIAMENT

For eight days, from December 1 – 8, 1999, seven thousand delegates from 90 nations attended 800 lectures and meetings at a dozen different sites. A complex of shuttle buses moved people around the city for sixteen hours a day. In addition to the workshops, there were exhibits and art galleries, a week of films from around the world, photography and technology displays. The printed program was a substantial 240–page book in its own right.

The most impressive ceremonial occasions were the plenary sessions. The first of these was on December 1, World Aids Day, and it featured a dedication of the Aids Quilt and an address by the American, Cleve Jones, who originated the quilt project. Africa is the continent most devastated by Aids; indeed, 60% of teenagers in South Africa alone are HIV positive.

A second event was the procession through the streets of Cape Town. Delegates were dressed in striking colors, carried banners with quotations, calligraphy and symbols from their sacred books and traditions, chanted ancient melodies and used musical instruments of every shape and texture. Fundamentalists from varied religious groups lined the streets denouncing the Parliament and proclaiming that there was only one way to be religious, their way.

The formal opening ceremonies followed the procession.

A fourth significant event was the plenary session with Nelson Mandela. And the final one was the closing session with the Dalai Lama. I shall return to these last two speakers later.

I attended thirty lectures during the six days given to presentations. I returned with 63 pages of notes. There were individual sessions of great merit.

The Indian Ambassador to the European Union and the United Nations, Dr. N. P. Jain, spoke of a culture of non–violence. Other sessions dealt with a report from participants in a six–year Buddhist–Christian dialogue; still others explored the basic teachings of varied religious traditions.

There were social justice seminars and global ethics workshops as well as meetings on human rights, human responsibilities, and the Earth Charter.

I found a two–day symposium on science and religion especially productive. Internationally recognized scientists, theologians, professors and science writers for the *New York Times* and Public Broadcasting addressed the audience and debated with one another.

Throughout the symposium and, indeed, the Parliament, a commitment to interdisciplinarity was clear. The assumption was that encountering different mind–sets and diverse cognitive cultures engenders creativity and expansive horizons. It was intriguing to hear scholars from Asia, not shaped by Judaeo–Christian, Greco–Roman influences, dialogue with scholars from America and Europe who stress reason and choice in ways less congenial to Asian self–definition. As the world becomes a smaller place in terms of time and space, it has become a larger arena for the human mind and spirit. Less and less is alien in this new world of a dawning third millennium.

TWENTIETH–CENTURY ICONS

Nelson Mandela's talk on December 5 was, perhaps, the stellar event of the Parliament. He was received with extraordinary enthusiasm and given the Gandhi–King Award for Non–Violence by Mahatma Gandhi's granddaughter, Ela Gandhi.

Mandela was imprisoned for 18 of his 28 years on Robben Island, seven nautical miles off the coast of Cape Town. Delegates gathered on Robben Island one morning in a ceremony of dedication, prayer, and speeches.

The Island had a notoriety about it on a par with Devils Island and

Alcatraz. It had once been a leper colony, then an asylum for the mentally ill, and finally a place for hardened criminals and political prisoners.

Political prisoners were treated harshly, humiliated, tortured, and permitted to see their families only twice a year and to write no more than two letters of five pages each per year. The inhumanity of it all is overwhelming when it is seen concretely. Mandela's lack of bitterness and vengeance after decades of cruelty rises to the level of religious importance in its own right.

"We have significant cause to be cynical about humanity," he observed." "But this gathering counters despairing cynicism and reaffirms the nobility of the human spirit."

"We commend," he continued, "the Parliament of World Religions for its immense role in saying the common ground is greater and more enduring than those aspects which divide."

Religion, he claimed, "was one of the motivating factors in bringing down apartheid." Religions "bought land, built and equipped schools, found teachers and paid them."

Without the Church and without religious institutions, Mandela noted, he would not be where he is now.

And, so, when he heard of the Parliament, "I changed my plans because nothing has been more important to South Africa than religion...all religions...Religion sustained us through all the years in jail. Religion is a mighty force."

Such a marvelous transformation, from Robben Island to the Presidency of South Africa; from imprisonment to the Nobel Peace Prize.

The Dalai Lama addressed the Parliament in the closing plenary session. He considers the Parliament important and was instrumental in re–creating the Parliament again in 1993 after a century's hiatus.

He spoke of caring for others as the surest means to tranquillity with ourselves.

We must not, he insisted, propagate our traditions but, rather, learn how to make them contribute to the better world and enriched humanity we all want.

There are, he added, two spiritualities possible for us, one built on religious faith and one which makes no reference to it. Both have their validity. Furthermore, even if we affirm religious faith we should not dissipate our energy in prayer and meditation when action on behalf of others is the urgent need. Quite a statement from a Buddhist leader whose life is given to contemplation!

The Dalai Lama's humor, informality and respect for others form a message of telling eloquence.

Two people, one from the political world, Nelson Mandela, the other, identified with a major religious tradition, the Dalai Lama, joined common ground in the Parliament. They spoke to the common decency of the human heart and put their faith in the potential humanity has to make a world fit for the presence of life in it. Neither neglected religion or politics since religion is always somehow political. Mahatma Gandhi once observed that the spiritual search passes through the political order. Conversely, politics in its best expression has a religious resonance. To liberate people from the concrete circumstances which make them suffer and imprison their future is the goal of all religious traditions and of everything that is authentic in the political order.

The Parliament of World Religions is a gathering place for the human family. It offers a global ethic on which we can be united and an earth charter through which all life on the planet is given a chance. To proceed without ethics or without ecological sensitivity is to doom the human family. All good political leaders know this. And every religious leader, worthy of the name, knows this as well.

The Parliament gives us confidence for another millennium of life. It is the best way I know of to bring the second millennium to a close and to open a door for another thousand years of hope.

7

A BRIEF, LIBERAL CATHOLIC DEFENSE OF ABORTION

Daniel A. Dombrowski and Robert Deltete
(University of Illinois Press, 2000)

In a brilliant new book, Daniel A. Dombrowski and Robert Deltete, professors of philosophy at Seattle University, argue that the Catholic tradition on abortion is very different indeed from the present teaching of the Catholic Church. They explore this issue through two different philosophies and two major Catholic theologians.

The different philosophies are the ontological (the fetus as person) and perversity of sex (abortion distorts sex) philosophies. Augustine is primarily identified with the perversity of sex argument and Aquinas with the ontological approach.

The authors begin with Augustine and demonstrate quite convincingly that Augustine made a sharp distinction between early and late abortions. He condemned abortion in both instances but for different reasons.

In the early stages, abortion is evil, not because human life is present but because the purpose of sex is destroyed. It is clear that Augustine did not believe human life is present from conception. He says he does not know when the life in the womb is human (ignoro quando incipiat homo in utere vivere). He assumes that "unformed abortions persih like seeds that have never been fructified." It is not the loss of human life or a person which grieves Augustine but the loss of the purpose of sex.

For Augustine sex had value only if it intended procreation. It was, nonetheless, always sinful, even for spouses seeking to have children unless they managed to have sex without pleasure. Pleasure vitiated sex which was already corrupt in its essence. The best way to deal with sex was to abstain from it.

Only procreation could allow sex some limited meaning. Augustinian principles eventually condemn contraception, the rhythm method, post–menopausal sex and sex for sterile couples. Abortion in the early stages is evil because it destroys the conception which was the only purpose of sex. Abortion in the later stages is evil because there is human life present after sensation and quickening occur.

Even conservative theologians today reject Augustine's analysis of sex and his reasons for condemning early abortion.

It is instructive to note that Augustine presupposes a development of human life in the womb and not an immediate identification of conception and ensoulment.

AQUINAS

Aquinas is less interested in abortion than Augustine. There is no article in the *Summa* on abortion. Thomas develops the ontological argument. Technically called hylomorphism, it states that there is no human life in the womb until the fifth or sixth month when quickening occurs. Until then we are dealing with vegetative life and animal life, both of which are produced by human semen and both of which cease to exist when the fetus attains full sensation and a human form. It is then that a rational soul is infused into the fetus from without and by God.

God cannot infuse a soul into a small cluster of cells because body and soul belong together; a cluster of cells is not a human body. Aquinas believes in delayed hominization. Indeed hylomorphism is essential to his philosophy and his definition of what it means to be human. Two subsequent ecumenical councils (Vienne in 1311 and Trent in 1545) taught that no human embryo could have a human soul.

SEVENTEENTH CENTURY SCIENCE

Dombrowski and Deltete assign the change in Catholic thinking to two developments, one in the seventeenth century and the other in the nineteenth. For more than a millenium the Catholic tradition worked with assumptions and teaching it now rejects.

In the seventeenth century, magnifying glasses and, later, microscopes detected what appeared to be a human form in fetal tissue. The time of ensoulment was, accordingly, pushed back to the moment of conception or soon after this.

Twentieth century science would precise the early appearance of a human form more accurately. There may be sense receptors and brain cells present, fairly early on. But they are more like a collection of loose wires and switches. They are not connected until about the fifth or sixth month when a cerebral cortex is in place. It is then that we have a human form and human perception.

The time line for a radical change in the development of the fetus around the fifth or sixth month is astonishingly the same in Scholasticism, science and the Supreme Court's Roe versus Wade decision.

NINETEENTH CENTURY DOCTRINE

The authors argue that a different boundary was crossed in the nineteenth century when Pius IX, in 1854, defined the Immaculate Conception as a dogma of faith. If Mary was conceived without sin, it was now argued, she must have been a person from her conception. One cannot attribute sin to vegetative or animal life.

Fifteen years after this, in 1869, Pius IX, for the first time in Church history, excommunicated all those directly involved in abortions with no distinction between early or late abortions. Indeed, even the preservation of the life of the mother was not a sufficient reason for an abortion once conception was in place.

The stage was set for a holy crusade against abortion because the volatile elements of human life, marian piety, papal loyalty and permissive sexuality and even feminine autonomy were in place.

No book is perfect but this book is excellent.

There are times when Dombrowki and Deltete sound almost harshly rational in their brilliant and unrelenting analysis. The tears and trauma of abortion are not given place in this book.

There are other moments in the book when the logical options are not complete. The authors will argue about issues like the potentiality of life without detailing the possibility of a tertium quid in the alternatives they delineate.

A future edition of the book might be more ecologically sensitive. At times the sense of respect for varied dimensions of inanimate and non–human existence is not operative. The eagerness of the authors to limit moral claims to sentient life, quite well argued, gives the impression that creation is less comprehensively sacred than they intend. The ecological sacramentality of creation would enhance the value of this book in my opinion.

I would have preferred to have some development of the pastoral, theological, and spiritual consequences of the authors' positions. In fairness to them, however, they are philosophers and have every right to limit their focus as they did.

Dembrowski and Deltete are insightful and fair throughout their book. They have done their research. This book is a model of reasoned discourse about an inflammatory issue. I cannot think of a Catholic or thoughtful person who would not benefit from it.

8

REFLECTIVE COMPASSION

There are two wrenching decisions abortion imposes upon us; its legality and its morality.

The legality of abortion, I believe, is an irreversible decision in global, contemporary life. I do not believe the vast majority of people, their legislatures, voters, and judges are obtuse and insensitive. I see grace and goodness in the decision by the world at large to deal with, perhaps, the most traumatic and heart breaking of human decisions. I feel compassion, as most people do, for the unborn child and for the helpless woman. Both deserve our tears.

The general consensus in America and among American Catholics is sound. If I understand it rightly, it goes like this: Americans favor abortion rights and disapprove of abortion. It should be permitted but discouraged. The issue is too private, too personal, too much tied up with faith and personal freedom for the government to regulate abortion totally by law. Indeed, such laws are unenforceable. There would be a national trauma every time a woman was arrested and put in jail for having had an abortion.

America has permitted legal abortion not to protect the health of the mother or child, but as a constitutional right. It is privacy and protection from government which is the essence of the American decision on the legality of abortion. The fetus is not a person under law in the American legal scheme of things. The woman is. Nonetheless, the Supreme Court reminds us that a woman's right to abortion is not unlimited (nor is freedom of speech for that matter) and that a woman cannot be isolated from the broader community in which she resides.

This legal situation is about as clear as it is likely to get. Once again, people prove reliable. Americans seem to have gotten the legal status of abortion right: permit it but remain sensitive to the trauma and heartache.

The second question on abortion concerns its morality. The essence of the moral decision rests on the fact that we cannot be sure that the fetus is a person until birth or viability. Christian and Jewish tradition reflect that ambiguity. The *Mishnah* speaks of a fetus becoming a person when the head or greater part is born. The two greatest Christian theologians, Augustine and St. Thomas Aquinas, believed that a fetus is not a person until it has human form in the womb. Indeed, until the end of the eighteenth century, the Catholic Church prohibited baptizing an aborted fetus if it did not have a human shape to it. In any case, there is no formal funeral service for a fetus as there is for a•deceased child who has been born.

Official church teaching is adamant at the moment on the evil of abortion. Official church teaching, however, has changed dramatically in other areas in the past. Consider: salvation of non–Catholics and non–Christians; slavery; inquisitions and torture; ecumenism; worship in the language people understand; divorce and remarriage. The number of Catholics in the United States who believe abortion is immoral in all instances is about 19 percent. The American Catholic conviction seems to be this: it is very important to value life in the womb from the earliest stages, but one must do so conditionally.

Abortion, therefore, is always tragic, but not always immoral. Nothing is intelligible outside its history; therefore, one must look to all the circumstances. Error may have no rights but people do. Even if a woman chooses incorrectly according to an abstract standard, she may choose morally in the vortex of competing claims and values she faces when making a complex, lonely, devastating decision.

And, so, it is not easy. And perhaps will never be, no matter how one decides. Dialogue on abortion and legal rights seems correct to me. No one need have an abortion simply because dialogue and legal rights exist.

In any case, there are good women and men on both sides of this dilemma. This is so because the issue is not simple, legally or morally. In such a climate, infallible pronouncements and condemnations of women are insensitive. It is more likely that people will hear teaching from a church that does not work for legal force and punishments but addresses, instead, the conscience of the nation and of women.

The Catholic Church once endorsed slavery, even though the evidence that slaves were human was overwhelming. It should, therefore be sensitive to the ambiguities involved in abortion, where questions of the humanity of the fetus and the rights of the woman are much more difficult to settle.

If the Catholic Church wishes to have compassion for its wrong decisions in the past and to take into account the complex circumstances it labored under in making them, then, surely, such a church can understand how difficult it might be for women to know always what love requires and what is right. Jesus asked for love even in the uneasy situations where love is not expected. Is it too much to hope that the church which came from him might reflect his compassion and sensitivity?

Hope In Ministry

If you believe in the Word of God, you don't fail.
You dance a little, cry a little, sing a new song —
      share a word, hug a friend, dream at night,
      break bread, take new wine,
      careful to throw out the old wineskins
      and you don't fail.
You may have only five loaves and a few fish
    and it seems so little when
    there is so much to be done.
You may have only six jars of water
    and no one is very happy with you or with that.
You may have only a mustard seed or a manger.
The only way out may be Egypt.
You may have only three years to do it all in.
You might not even have a boat of your own.
You may have only a few stories—no title, no degree,
    no Temple to back you up or to support you.
You may have only the road to Jerusalem
 and it goes uneasily through Samaria.

You may have only bread and a cup of wine
  on the night before it's all over.
You may have only a few friends and they're all asleep.
You may not have the right words to get yourself off the charge—
and so you forgive them for not knowing
  what else to do with you.
You may not even have a Father in the darkness of Calvary
  and wish your mother weren't there.
You may have only one apostle left at the cross
  and hardly any disciples.
Sometimes all you've got are your wounds and
  the last shred of hope.
But if the Word of God is in you—you win—
     not for your sake alone but for everyone.
If the Word of God is with us, nothing is lost,
  not even a coin,
  certainly not a sheep that wants to be rescued
  or a minister who seeks to be a shepherd.
Nothing is lost
          not even Peter who denies Christ
          or the Pharisee who comes to him only at night.
Nothing is lost.
Once the church had only the Word of God, nothing else,
  and it proclaimed its message without power or legal sanction in
Jerusalem, Athens and Rome.
Astonishingly, it prevailed—with the Word of God alone—
     this is not rhetoric—it is history.
We have the Word of God.

Why do we keep thinking we need anything else?

United Nations
Papers

10

The Vatican and the Catholic Consensus on Population

There were seven insights where the Catholic Tradition would have strengthened the United Nations Cairo Document on Population:

1. Marriage should have been cited as a privileged place for sexual experience and children.
2. The observation might have been made that human rights can drift into individualism and selfishness unless they are balanced with human responsibility and ethical concerns.
3. A too ready access to contraception can give a message that sexual activity is a health issue rather than a moral one as well.
4. Sexual maturity is not achieved by rescuing people from the consequences of their own irresponsibility by technological or medical procedures.
5. Motherhood is a special human event which deserves social support.
6. Coercion vitiates reproductive and sexual rights and is not a human and ethical solution to the population question. (Cairo dealt with this but less fully than it might have.)
7. Abortion is a traumatic experience for many women.

If there are valuable insights, why do so many Catholics and so many people of good will resist a Catholic influence in sexual ethics?

I believe this is due to two problems.
The first of these is rigidity. Let us follow the seven points in part one and indicate the liabilities of the Catholic position.

1. Marriage is a privileged place...but the Church is frequently harsh and cruel with those who do not go in this direction.
2. Human rights can drift into individualism...but community and tradition drift just as often into tyranny.
3. Sexual activity has a moral dimension...but the guilt, shame, and censure which are fostered are frequently excessive.
4. Sexual maturity is not achieved by rescuing people from consequences...but neither is it responsible to expose people needlessly to death and unwanted pregnancies.
5. Motherhood is a special human event...but it is not the defining element for femininity any more than fatherhood defines masculinity.
6. The Vatican concern with coercive abortion and contraception can itself become coercive if abortion and contraception are denied to all citizens of every country by force of law and with legal punishments as the Vatican wishes. Indeed this legal solution to abortion intimidates people and prevents many from hearing the Vatican clearly when it has helpful insights to offer. No one, after all, is compelled to choose abortion or contraception merely because they are legal. In any case, the Church is free to witness against abortion and contraception as ethical choices even if they are legally and civilly an option.
7. Abortion will never be eliminated by law. There is an irreversible world consensus which supports it and this consensus comes from Catholic countries, cultures and citizens. Indeed, one might argue that abortion should not be eliminated by law since this deprives people of the choice to refuse abortion freely, morally, and in conscience. Conscience and morality demand that the person be free and informed. The Vatican

concern with the trauma and heart–ache of abortion is not heard by the world community because there is a suspicion that this concern will be manipulated into an argument for legal prohibitions.

People disturbed by the Vatican approach to reproductive rights are often troubled because these decisions are reached without the participation of all but a few voices, none of them feminine and none of them from married people. Such Vatican decisions are not, therefore, truly Catholic decisions but papal decisions or oligarchical decisions.

SHOULD THE VATICAN HAVE ENDORSED THE CAIRO CONSENSUS?

The Cairo document resonates with themes the Catholic Church proclaims:

1. Excessive consumption degrades the planet, impoverishes the human family and deprives people of life.
2. The human person, sexual and reproductive rights are more important than markets and demographics in population control.
3. Education and choice enable women to become directors of their own lives, possessors of their own bodies, and moral actors in their own sexual histories.
4. The poor, especially poor women and children, have a special claim on our compassion.

These extremely important values did not lead the Vatican to endorse Cairo enthusiastically because of Cairo's unwillingness to condemn contraception and abortion in every instance, a condemnation that was to be so absolute that there was to be no exception for the life of the mother, rape, incest or AIDS infection.

Let us look at these issues more closely and suggest how the Vatican might have adopted a more nuanced approach on contraception and abortion.

Cairo was concerned about public safety and reproductive health; the Vatican could have favored both without morally endorsing contraception and abortion.

Cairo made it clear that abortion should not be promoted, that it is never to be coercive and must always be safe. The Vatican could have affirmed these values without compromising its position on contraception and abortion.

There is admittedly some risk in endorsing conditions under which abortion should go forward in those countries where it is legal and at the same time declaring one's moral objections to abortion. Such risk is built into the process of negotiation and participation in a global declaration. If the Vatican had no intention of changing its positions, it should not have entered the process. It was clear to all that the Vatican had no chance of bringing the world community to declare abortion illegal and immoral everywhere. Had the Vatican been more resilient and creative, it would have gained greater credibility and would have given its message a better possibility of being heard.

Cairo called for full and equal rights for men and women. The argument might be made that women require recognition of their secular rights more urgently than men. This is so because women have been discounted and abused through history far more than men. Pregnancy, furthermore, imposes a graver burden on women.

Because of this, one might argue that there are no abiding women's rights without reproductive rights. If this is not granted, women are held in bondage to their biology. One might observe that natural family planing does not liberate women from this bondage. Responsible sexuality may have less to do with the means by which conception is prevented than it does with the intentions, motives and behavior of the couple. One would like to hear more from the Vatican about this.

CONCLUSION

The Gospels are far more focused on condemning dominative power over others than on sexual behavior. The Vatican reverses these priorities and speaks seldom, if ever, about dominative power over others in the Church and in marriage. This power is never condemned with the vehemence directed at contraception and abortion.

It is clear that people at large do not see the Catholic Church as the world's best hope for women's rights. This might have changed somewhat at Cairo had the Vatican been more attentive to women as human beings rather than as reproductive agents.

The impression given at Cairo is that the Vatican views the world suspiciously and does not grant it moral and ethical wisdom. Yet, the human family progressed through a million years of evolution without the Church; even now eighty five percent of the world is not Catholic and yet handles life with integrity and grace.

The Vatican finds it even more difficult to admit that it learns from the world. Yet, the world took the lead in abolishing slavery, ending censorship, terminating inquisitions, calling for the end to capital punishment. The world, well before the Church, promoted democracy, ecology and women's rights. And the world has gained much from the Church: the Gospels and the proclamation of Jesus Christ; monasticism and spiritual theology; a message on compassion, mercy and forgiveness. One might continue but the point is made.

If the Vatican has taught the world that life is valued conditionally, so that one could kill a human being in self–defense, war, and capital punishment, with the Church's full approval, why is it so difficult for the Vatican to view abortion conditionally? If we can kill human beings if the context is right, why is the context never right for a fetus? The same Vatican which insists there is human life at conception does not act in its worship life as though this is the case. It imposes no necessity to baptize a fetus and it does not offer a fetus burial rituals. So, there are some differences and some conditions which make a difference.

Can we be sure, then, can the Vatican be sure, that Cairo had nothing to teach the Catholic Church about women's rights and reproductive rights?

11

CATHOLICS AND
THE CAIRO CONSENSUS

MAKING JUDGMENTS

Allow me to begin by sharing with you three quotations:

"People are the most important and valuable resource of any nation."

"…eradicating poverty (is) an indispensable requirement."

"The developed countries (must)…narrow imbalances in a manner that can benefit all countries, particularly the developing countries."

If one did not know the sources, one might assume that such statements came from a document of a major world religion. In actual fact, the quotations come from the United Nations Cairo Document on Population, principles 2, 7, and 15 respectively.

These statements are not untypical. The Cairo document has a religious resonance. It is disappointing that the Vatican did not celebrate this achievement of the world community.

SEEING PROBLEMS

The Vatican seems particularly concerned with three aspects of the Cairo document. It would prefer a different approach in each of the following areas:

▶ Sexuality must be responsible.

▶ Abortion is immoral and should be illegal.

▶ A reproductive rights approach drains scarce resources from human needs in developing countries.

Let us look at each of these concerns with full respect for the Vatican position and the Cairo document.

Sexuality must be responsible
The Vatican prefers, as I see it, a changed emphasis on:
- ▶ sexual education
- ▶ responsible parenthood
- ▶ sexual fidelity
- ▶ the unitive and procreative dimensions of sexual experience.

The Cairo document does indeed, I believe, develop the first three of these concerns in a way which should have led to Vatican endorsement. For example, the values approach to sexual education the Vatican rightly favors is present in the document if one is attentive to what Cairo says about the elimination of coercion, the dignity and rights of women, and sustainable development. All may not be there but a great deal is.

Cairo recognizes responsible parenthood by drawing attention to population considerations, the eradication of poverty, and development. It does not apply the principle of responsible parenthood as directly to the consciences of the couple as the Vatican does but it makes a beginning.

Sexual fidelity is suggested by the document's stress on the prior rights and needs of children and on the empowerment of women with all that implies for responsible relationships. Cairo might have developed this notion further but its approach is not unacceptable.

I suggest that the Vatican contribution was undermined by its excessive focus on contraception and abortion and by its didactic rather than dialogical approach. It missed a substantive opportunity to show itself as an ally rather than an adversary of women's rights.

The Cairo document did not deal with the link between the unitive and procreative character of sexual intercourse. This is a very useful Vatican insight. Greater acceptance of this concept, however, is impeded because the Vatican has not developed the consequences of its position fully and seems unwilling to hear the world at large on this issue.

Abortion is immoral and should be illegal
The Cairo document went as far as it could go to meet the concerns

of the Vatican and others with abortion. It states that abortion should not be promoted as a means of family planning and that it should be safe whenever it occurs. There was no possibility that the Vatican position could win adoption at the United Nations.

There are concerns a number of Catholics have with the Vatican. It does not, for example, speak as passionately about a mother's right to life as it does about that of unborn life. The Vatican emphasis on the family as central does not take sufficiently into account the tragedy a family faces when a pregnancy threatens the life of a mother. The Vatican sensitivity to the agony of the aborted fetus does not extend to the agony of bearing an unwanted child, one possibly conceived in rape and developing in a deformed manner.

Rights versus Needs

It is not helpful to pit needs against rights. If they do not work in tandem, the dignity of the persons is violated. Let us look at some examples.

- ▶ One should not give people food and shelter and not inform them that they have a right to these.
- ▶ The Vatican once insisted that the need of all people to become members of the one, true Church overrode their rights of conscience and religious freedom; Vatican Council II reversed this position in 1965.
- ▶ The needs of women have been met in patriarchal family settings but at a terrible cost to their rights.
- ▶ An excessive stress on needs portrays people as victims and indigent (which is partly true) but it neglects them as subjects of rights and moral agency.
- ▶ Rights derive from our very nature and, in terms of Cairo, from our sexual identity; needs become severe because the world is badly managed.
- ▶ In quite another vein, the Vatican failure to address the human rights of priests to marry has created catastrophic need and pastoral starvation in the Catholic community.
- ▶ In any case, unless women's rights are dealt with, women will always be needy.

I want the Catholic Church to be credible and I want the rich resources of its tradition and its life to benefit the human family. I offer some suggestions which I believe may prove helpful.

▶ The Vatican can become a more influential participant in the global dialogue on women and rights if it welcomes the Cairo document as essentially moral and religious; indeed, as an expression of the conscience of the world and of its good-will.

▶ Address attention not only to the anguish of abortion but to the anguish of women bearing unwanted pregnancies and feeling helpless in a world and in religious systems which frequently do not affirm them or recognize their rights

▶ Settle for the legality of abortion while preserving the right to argue against it morally, especially when it is used as a family planning alternative.

▶ Trust women at large and their preference to keep their children; legal abortion allows them to affirm their children even more strongly and freely because abortion becomes an alternative they themselves do not choose; this makes them willing participants in their own life.

▶ Become attentive to Catholic NGO's who represent not the Vatican position but the wide spectrum of opinion in the Catholic community; dialogue does not undermine one's position but shows its strength; the Catholic Church at large rejects major elements in the Vatican policy on sexual and reproductive rights and it does this by overwhelming majorities in many cases; this alternative view of such magnitude needs to be heard and respected.

▶ It is time to end the hostility engendered by seeing people with opposing viewpoints as adversaries and as badly motivated; we underestimate the intelligence and good will of the human family.

Allow me to end with this quote of Richard Niebuhr:

Frantic orthodoxy is never rooted in faith but in doubt.
It is when we are not sure that we are doubly sure.

12

A CALL TO ACCOUNTABLITY

Does a person lose human rights by accepting baptism and, even more, religious vows in the Catholic Church?

I think the answer is "yes;" not because baptism or religious vows, of themselves, require the forfeiting of such rights but because of changeable Church policies.

The trauma and abuse of nuns or women religious is connected, I believe, with the wide-spread denial of human rights in the Catholic Church.

The negation of human rights is linked essentially with the system of clerical and male domination of all aspects of Church life, especially over laity and particularly over women.

When this system causes agony that the Vatican clearly did not intend, it is not enough for the Vatican to apologize. The system itself must be dismantled; it has no biblical warrant; it wounds innocent people unbearably. Apologies are not sufficient. Women have been battered by apologies from abusers who do not change their behavior from time immemorial.

The nullification of human rights in the Catholic Church manifests itself in five areas:

▶ *There is a denial, in the Catholic Church, of reproductive rights.*

Some, after vows, are refused the right to marry and have children with threats of punishment, social shame, and loss of livelihood.

Even when it is clear to people of good will that the system of mandatory celibacy is not working (pedophilia, HIV infection, concubinage, shortage of pastors, desire of most Catholics for change), the Vatican maintains this mandatory, abusive, destructive system.

In the United Nations, especially at Conferences in Cairo and Beijing, the Vatican obstructs the availability of contraceptives that would give women relief from mandatory pregnancy and disease.

▶ *There is a denial, in the catholic church, of gender equity.*

The inferior status of women in the Catholic Church is decreed by doctrine and law. On the basis of gender alone, women are excluded from all offices of decisive significance, from a final voice in their own affairs, from all judicial decisions which are always made for them or against them, never by them.

▶ *There is a denial, in the catholic church, of governmental accountability.*

There is no right to have a meaningful voice in holding leaders accountable. Leadership, by decree, doctrine, and law, rests on an absolute, papal monarchy. This system is limited to males alone. Papal monarchy defines itself as infallible; decides, on its own, that it enjoys life-time tenure; and permits neither recourse nor appeal from any of its decisions (Canon Law, 333). This governance has no endorsement from the Gospel or apostolic tradition. It functions against the preferences of a vast majority of Catholics. We believe it harms the credibility of the papacy and its capacity to heal the divisions in our Church.

▶ *There is a denial, in the catholic church, of due process.*

The prosecuter is jury and judge in the Catholic Church. Women's concerns, furthermore, are represented by men alone in a process which is secret, in which accusers are never named and from which there is no appeal.

▶ *There is a denial, in the catholic church, of free speech and assembly.*

Even issues which affect women critically, the right to be ordained, the definition of their own sexuality, their role in society at large, all this is decided by men. Women are forbidden by papal policy to discuss these issues in any public forum, no matter how learned their voices or how devoted their service to the Church and people. The prohibition on discussion of ordination is articulated with threats and warnings as was recently the case at the Womens Ordination International Conference in Dublin, Ireland.

Does a person lose human rights by accepting baptism and, even more, religious vows, in the catholic church?

The answer is "yes."

Why is this done?

To create a system of domination by clerics and men over laity and women.

How is this done?

By a denial of reproductive rights, gender equity, accountability, due process, free speech and assembly.

What is the result?

The confinement of women to a lay state and the abuse of women, whether intended or not. This abuse seeks to control women's sexuality and thinking. It seeks to make them silent conspirators in their own oppression. It gives them no means by which to redress their grievances. The abuse is sometimes, whether intended or not, so massive that it robs them of their dignity, their rights, and their lives.

That all this is done in the name of Christ amounts to an abuse not only of women but of the Gospel itself.

13

CATHOLICS AND CONSCIENCE

Catholics overwhelmingly support the use of condoms to prevent AIDS infection. Depending on the specific study, the percentages reach virtual unanimity. Yet Catholic official teaching remains divided.

There are three questions at the heart of this issue.

HOW DO WE PROMOTE MATURE SEXUALITY?

All religious communities endorse mature sexuality. It is at the core of the Global Ethic promulgated by the Parliament of World Religions.

Sexual development and maturity are the means by which life is transmitted and nurtured. Indeed, self–respect and human rights are intimately connected with the way sexuality is defined, expressed and made responsible.

Religious leaders around the world agree that sexual maturity cannot be achieved only by making sex safe, by preventing disease, by improving the technology of contraception. Maturity requires attitudes of respect, responsibility and rights which transcend the concrete conditions of sexual behavior. Indeed, it might be argued that unless these prior attitudes are in place, even safe sex may be an assault on the dignity of others.

Catholic church leaders tend to support the distribution of prophylactics when there is an educational program that underlines church teaching on responsible sexuality. Thus, Monsignor Jacques Suaudeau of the Vatican's Pontifical Council for the Family writes in *L'Osservatore*

Romano, the official Vatican newspaper, that "the use of prophylactics" in some circumstances, "is actually a lesser evil but it cannot be proposed as a model of humanization and development" (April 19, 2000).

The French Bishops Council declared in 1996 that the use of condoms "can be understood in the case of people for whom sexual activity is an ingrained part of their life style and for whom [that activity] represents a serious risk; but it has to be firmly added that such a method does not promote mature sexuality."

The German Bishops Conference issued a document in 1993 which affirmed that "human conscience constitutes the decisive authority in personal ethics." They add that "consideration must be given to the high number of abortions among single mothers and the spread of suffering even if the underlying behavior cannot be condoned in many cases…"

Ranking church leaders, in individual statements, support the use of contraceptives in the context of responsible sexuality and prevention of AIDS.

The Cardinal Archbishop of Paris, Jean–Marie Lustiger, declared in 1989 that love and chastity were essential values in sexual maturity but that if a person is "HIV positive" and "cannot live in chastity" that such a person "should use the means that have been proposed" to prevent infection of others.

Bishop Eugenio Rixen of Goias, Brazil, adds that the principle of the lesser of two evils makes the "use of condoms less serious, morally speaking, than getting infected or infecting other people with the AIDS virus" (June, 2000).

Most people would be astonished to hear that ninety percent of the theologians on the papal birth control commission, at the conclusion of the Second Vatican Council, maintained that artificial birth control is not intrinsically evil and that official teaching against contraception could be changed.

HOW DO WE SAVE LIVES?

The Catholic tradition is more resilient than many realize when issues of human life and dignity are compelling.

For most of its history, the Church condemned cremation severely as a violation of the dignity of the human body and an attack on the central Catholic doctrine of the resurrection of the body. It felt so strongly on this issue that a Catholic funeral service was forbidden to all who would choose cremation. Even in those centuries, however, cremation was not only allowed but also considered a moral duty in times of Plague when infection and the lives of others were at issue.

Catholic doctrine forbidding usury or the taking of interest on money continued through its history. Usury is condemned in the Bible and it was affirmed by centuries of Catholic teaching. Yet, when it was clear that the new economic order of the modern period depended on usury for the financial health of the human family, the imputation of interest on money loaned was not only deemed permissible for the world at large but became the norm for the Vatican banking system itself.

Catholic teaching on a just war theory prevailed without significant challenge from the time of Augustine in the fifth century until the twentieth century. Just war theory maintains that there are legitimate and even moral reasons for engaging in war provided that war is a last resort, that proportionate and not excessive means are used and that non–combatants are protected. The advent of nuclear weapons has changed Catholic thinking in this area. Nuclear war is seen as unjust because proportionality and the indiscriminate killing of innocent people, even of the planet, have changed the moral equation. The protection of life, perhaps of all life, has led Catholic leaders to conclude that the very possession of nuclear weapons is morally questionable. The United States Catholic Bishops wrote in their 1983 pastoral letter, "The Challenge of Peace," that there must be a "completely fresh appraisal of war" and that it was irresponsible "simply to repeat what we have said before." Nuclear war was deemed immoral; the possession of nuclear weapons was considered tentatively moral only as an interim measure to minimize the threat of a nuclear holocaust and as a step "on the way toward progressive disarmament."

The consistent thinking of the Catholic church has affirmed the lesser of two evils. This approach reasons that the ambiguity of choices sometimes makes it necessary to prefer one evil in order to prevent a greater evil. Thus, a pregnant woman may choose the removal of a cancerous uterus even if it entails the death of the fetus because the intention is the preservation of her life. It accepts the "evil" of the termination of prenatal life as a lesser evil, not intended directly.

A terminally ill patient may choose to forego all surgery and life support systems and permit death long before its biological inevitability as the lesser of evils. The "evil" of choosing one's own death is seen as the lesser of evils when the alternative is prolonged, painful, and pointless continuation of life, achieved only through extraordinary methods.

The AIDS crisis claims more human lives than Plague or nuclear weapons took in their history. The crisis has the potential to destabilize world financial systems, with consequent malnourishment and the death of millions not infected with AIDS. The economic crisis is as severe as the usury crisis of former centuries. Yet contraception is not condemned in the Bible; usury was explicitly forbidden there. If a biblical prohibition can be set aside when conditions change substantially, a non–biblical prohibition can even more readily be reversed when the consequences of human lives and the lesser evil are weighed in the balance.

The Catholic church cannot and will not promote a "culture of death" if the lives of tens of millions of people can be saved through the moral choices open to the Catholic tradition.

We have reached a point with contraception and AIDS where the intent is no longer the prevention of pregnancy but the prevention of death. Contraception in the context we are considering is not aimed at controlling population but at avoiding a holocaust.

HOW DO WE LIVE IN A WORLD THAT IS LESS THAN IDEAL?

The Catholic church is convinced that an action that is intrinsically evil, corrupt to its very roots, cannot be utilized as a moral means even in a lesser of two evils approach. Thus, one may not kill innocent civilians to win a war even over an evil system such as Nazism. One may not control population growth with infanticide or forced abortion. One may not order the rape of women in order to demoralize the enemy and hasten the end of a war.

Contraception, therefore, can only be universally prohibited if it is deemed intrinsically evil.

The encyclical letter of Pope Paul VI, *Humanae Vitae* (1968), prohibited all means of artificial contraception. The pope, however, made it clear that this teaching was not infallible. He could not have done this unless there was doubt about the intrinsic evil of contraception.

Indeed, the papal commission on birth control could not have been summoned, previous to the encyclical, unless there was doubt about the intrinsic evil of contraception.

The vast majority of Catholics and of priests see no intrinsic evil in contraception. Indeed, immediately after the publication of *Humanae Vitae*, the official Catholic pastoral letters of national bishops conferences in Belgium, Canada, France, Germany, the Netherlands, and the United States made it clear that there were instances when the conscience of a Catholic prevails against the papal prohibition. A couple, even though respecting the pope's teaching, might conclude that the need to limit births and the need to preserve the sexual life of a marriage might prompt them, in conscience, to choose contraception as the lesser of the evils.

Catholic theologians went further and considered instances where contraception was not the lesser of two evils but a value in its own right, provided that it fostered sexual maturity and responsibility.

The instances and examples we have cited happened long before there was an AIDS crisis, even before AIDS existed.

In the light of the magnitude of death before us, in the context of entire nations of orphan children and indeed of cultures whose young people are substantially absent, a new approach is imperative. Catholicism can find in its resources and in its commitment to life the resiliency to allow and recommend condom use to prevent a sexual plague more catastrophic than the bubonic death which almost destroyed European civilization.

The world does not always allow us to live in an ideal environment and according to our preferred wishes. It does demand of us, however, that we do live in the world and that we do so responsibly and generously. To stop AIDS is a life decision, a responsible choice, a generous action. When all efforts to promote mature sexuality are in place, we must also factor in the reality that all people are not mature. The realism of the Catholic tradition knows this and provides for this in other instances. Condoms to prevent AIDS can be a step on the way of teaching sexual maturity and responsibility. In the light of this, there is sufficient evidence that Catholics at large and leaders in increasing numbers affirm life over death and the protection of the innocent from the plague of AIDS.

Milestones
5 Early
Essays

14

BROKEN PROMISES

Over the years, since the first wave of resignations from canonical priesthood began, until the present, most of the issues inhibiting optional celibacy have been addressed and resolved. Obligatory celibacy has now lost the support of Scripture, Tradition, history, pastoral life and the minds and hearts of God's People. It is not only the breadth of this movement for a married priesthood, in terms of tens of thousands of priests and millions of laity, but the depth of this phenomenon, which is impressive.

It seems to me, however, that one issue has not been addressed sufficiently. It is often wielded by the official Church as a weapon to create insecurity in the resigned priest and suspicion of the priest in the larger community of the Church and even beyond the Church.

This insecurity has led many resigned priests to doubt their worth, to feel a sense of shame about who they are and what they have chosen, to wonder if God still loves them, to hesitate about continuing their ministry with people who are in need. They suppose they have not the right, the credentials, the support of God's favor to be identified as priests for those who require them to be precisely that.

Although many resigned married priests have come to believe they have acted in accord with biblical and pastoral norms, they feel accused and vilified in their consciences and in the convictions others have been encouraged to have about them.

The issue I am referring to is whether married priests are men of broken promises. Are they people who have abandoned their most sacred commitments, men whose word is no longer trustworthy, Christians who do not deserve to be entrusted with ministry because they have betrayed it, selfish individuals who prefer their own interests to the needs of communities for which they were ordained and consecrated?

The official Church tells the Christian Community at large, Catholic as well as Protestant, that resigned married priests deserve to be punished and marginalized for the sake of God's People, for the well-being of the Church, for the protection of Christ's Spirit in our communities. Even when former Episcopal priests are allowed to function as newly ordained married canonical Catholic priests, Rome and the American Bishops refuse this option to resigned priests who married after rather than before ordination. The reason given is that the former Episcopal priests have never broken a promise of celibacy they made to the Latin Rite Catholic Church. The commitments these Episcopal priests and selected other Protestant Pastors made to their own communities, their belief that they were once truly ordained there, is discounted.

The fact that resigned married priests made a far more serious commitment to be priests and to do ministry is not only dismissed by the official Church but, indeed, the Church terminates this most sacred of commitments even though the resigned priest never revokes it and offers himself for service time and again. His crime is his marriage, a marriage indeed, in most cases sacramental, a marriage in which the resigned priest may have demonstrated fidelity and love, sacrifice and courage, virtue and grace. The promise of celibacy is deemed more serious than priesthood or marriage, parenting and family life. Rome will gladly allow a resigned priest to function canonically and fully once again after a civil divorce or even if he abandons his wife and children provided that they are adequately provided for financially. This forsaking of an entire family is not seen as a broken promise since the marriage itself was viewed as an impediment to ministry even if the marriage happened to be sacramental.

Rome, of course, will think and act as it chooses. The question which concerns me is what this condemnation and rejection does to the heart of a married priest and to his family.

The purpose of my talk is to address this issue and to ask if Rome is right in its assessment. Or, if Rome is not, why so many married priests feel and act as though Rome were: I have less concern with persuading Rome to reconsider than I have hope that married priests and their families might be brought to a greater measure of peace by these remarks. I also believe that the fundamental goodness in the Catholic Church will prevail and that one day the Church will repent of this action, so unworthy of it, as it now repents of the Inquisition and the Crusades.

This essay is divided into four general topics:

▶ A Biblical Story
▶ A Conclusion (What is Commitment?)
▶ Three Questions
▶ Commitment as Terror and Commitment as Fidelity

A BIBLICAL STORY

The story is from the Book of Judges (11, 29–40).

Jephthah made a vow to the Lord. "If you give the Ammonites into my hands, then the first creature that comes out of the door of my house to meet me when I return in triumph from fighting shall be the Lord's and I will sacrifice it as a burnt offering."

Jephthah marched against the Ammonites to attack them and God delivered them into his power. It was a very severe defeat; with great slaughter the Ammonites were humiliated and crushed before the Israelites.

As Jephthah returned to his house, his daughter came out from it to meet him; she was dancing and playing the tambourine. This was his only child: apart from her he had neither son nor daughter. When he saw her, he tore his clothes and exclaimed, "Oh, my daughter, my heart is broken! Must it be you? I have made a solemn promise to God and I cannot break it. I cannot unsay what I have said."

She answered him: "My father, you have made a solemn promise to God. Deal with me as your vow demands."

"But grant me this one request," she said. "Give me two months to roam the hills and weep with my friends, because I will never marry."

"You may go," he said. She and her girl friends went up into the mountains and grieved because she was going to die and because she was compelled to be unmarried and childless.

After two months she came back to her father and he killed her since he had made a solemn promise to the Lord. She died unmarried and childless. He treated her as the vow he had uttered bound him.

This is why there is now a tradition in Israel. Every year the women of Israel gather to commemorate and to lament the slaughter of Jephthah's only daughter. They leave their homes and grieve for her for four days each year.

Allow me to make a few observations about this story.

There is a connection, I believe, between violence and rigid interpretation of promises and vows. We agree, of course, that promises and vows must be considered serious events and experiences in our lives. One's word should not be discounted as a trivial or frivolous commitment, as an obligation one might readily reject whenever something more to one's advantage or liking comes along. Nonetheless, the maintenance of a vow at all costs, with no adaptation or possibility of reversal is a militant and belligerent action. The connection in the story of Jephthah between armed conflict, human sacrifice and literal interpretation of the vow ought not to be lost on us.

We might ask ourselves what kind of a God does Jephthah's action imply? If Jephthah is right, God holds us to our word even if life is sacrificed to it. This is the essence of legalism in its worst possible connotation. Jephthah is so intent on keeping his word that all claims of human decency and compassion, all rights of others and alternative moral options are rejected. The law has literally killed the spirit. It is not only the life of Jephthah's daughter that is destroyed but the life of Jephthah himself who must forever live out in his remaining years the memory of the life he denied for the sake of his consistency with his own word.

There is more to the story. The worst of crimes and sins in Israel is idolatry. Although the Book of Judges does not label it as such, Jephthah has made an idol of his word and sacrificed his daughter to it.

It is significant that the passage ends with the community's grief. A venerable woman, a woman without a name or rights of her own, is sacrificed to the belligerent rigidity of a vow made by a man. The story is told poignantly. Jephthah's daughter is the only child he has. How much this story contrasts with the ministry of Jesus who calls back to life the daughter of Jairus, the synagogue official. "My little daughter is desperately sick. Do come and lay your hands on her to make her better and save her life" (Mark 5, 23). Luke tells us this was the only daughter Jairus had.

Or, consider the contrast with the widow of Naim who is burying her only son when Jesus rescues them. In both stories, Jesus violates the law for the sake of life; in both stories he heals rather than destroys a woman. On the way to Jairus' daughter, he is touched by a woman with a hemorrhage of blood; in the Naim story, he puts his hand on the bier of a dead man. Each of these instances entailed a legal impurity.

And, so, when we hold rigidly to our vows and promises, when we sacrifice life to legalism or even personal consistency, do we worship thereby the God of Jesus or the God of Jephthah?

When we worship the God of Jephthah, the community suffers. This story, almost a Greek tragedy in miniature, ends as the community mourns and laments for years the loss caused by a rigid interpretation of a promise. Have we learned anything from this?

AND A CONCLUSION (WHAT IS COMMITMENT?)

In the Jephthah story, the vow has become everything and life has become incidental to it. We might, of course, observe that the solution of this dilemma is not an approach to vows and one's word which trivializes them. Is there, we might ask, a middle ground, somewhere between rigidity and capriciousness?

There are three values which, I believe, justify a change from one's earlier word, indeed compel the change so that, if it is not made, one remains consistent with one's word, it is true, but not faithful to God or to the inner life of the Church.

The first of these values is life itself. It is exemplified in our story of Jephthah. We are obliged to reflect on whether consistency with an earlier promise enriches or diminishes our life and the lives of others. This is not always easy to determine but we know, at least, that the context for the right answer is not a promise we once made but the effect the continuance of the promise has on our own lives. To allow life to wither as promises are stalwartly maintained is an aberration.

The second of these values is a sense of integrity. If I remain consistent with my earlier promise, will I be true to what is deepest and most authentic in me? Has the Church or the institution or the other person who has received my promise been authentic in turn? If, for example, the official Church refuses to allow any discussion of the issue of obligatory celibacy, if it silences all honest and respectful dialogue, can one say the Church has acted with integrity and authenticity?

We might use another story to exemplify this point. After he wrote *Catch 22*, Joseph Heller wrote a novel, *Something Happened*, about Bobby Slocum. Slocum sacrifices his integrity by giving up his dreams and his freedom for the sake of a conventional life and corporate promotion. He becomes an utterly predictable person, willing to do whatever he is asked to do by the institution. Both he and the corporation realize that he is thoroughly dependable because he has absolutely no personal integrity. Slocum succeeds but at the price of his happiness and authenticity. His life vocation has been surrendered to the institution.

Integrity might be defined as consistency with our deepest longings and hopes. It is fidelity to the vocation we have been given to be ourselves. We must, of course, also be faithful to others; we shall consider that aspect of commitment in our third point.

Bobby Slocum needs institutional approval above all else. He cannot say "no" to an institution because he cannot say "yes" to himself.

If the Catholic Church one day allows priests to marry, certainly an option which is possible and even probable, will it then be honorable to marry and become inconsistent with one's former promise of celibacy? Is honor and integrity so totally in the control of an institution that the individual has no access to this on his or her own initiative?

The third of these values is intimacy. If I remain consistent with my earlier promise, must I keep others at a distance and significantly close off my emotional life? We might utilize a third story to make this point.

The main protagonist of Elia Kazan's *The Arrangement* is Eddie Anderson. He married a woman he does not love and becomes sexually active with a number of other women. He loses his capacity to feel anything with anyone and keeps his emotional life under strict control.

Intimacy is our vulnerability and sensitivity to others. It is the source of our compassion and our communion with others. This intimacy must not be so irresponsibly shared that one loses all capacity for one's integrity. But it must not be so thoroughly discounted that one is encouraged to be unaffected by the needs and the love of others for us. Clerical systems sometimes favor ideology over people, abstract ideals over relationships, promises of celibacy over commitment to others.

If we are to avoid the rigidity of Jephthah on the one hand and the self–indulgence of taking none of our promises seriously on the other, we need to measure the changes we make from our earlier promises by the effect this has on life, integrity and intimacy.

If the vows we have made are actually commitments to God, they remain stable as well as fluid. Thus, all I was as a priest in a canonical celibate system, I still am as a married priest but under a different formality. If, however, the vows I have made have been made, not to God but to an institution, then they are rigid and legalistic. In such an instance, I can only be faithful in a canonical system and I lose all I was by going forth from it.

The official Church senses this dilemma as it seeks to define a resigned married priest. It denies him the title of priest or cleric but knows he is not really a lay person because he has been ordained. It knows that something has gone on between us and God, between the Church and ourselves, in ordination, which cannot be annulled. And, so, it defines us as laity in reference to its canonical system but as priests in terms of its sacramental system and in terms of the commitments and promises we once made to ministry and never revoked. The commitment we made to God and people remains intact and complicates the canonical system of the Church which is incapable of dealing with us adequately. Indeed, the permission we were given or sought to marry sacramentally is the only impediment the Church cites to our continuing sacerdotal ministry.

One of the signs that I am not a committed person is the fact that I am constantly aware of how committed I am and of those who are not. When one is healthy, one does not speak endlessly of health. When one is happy, one does not feel a need to convince all others of how happy one is.

Commitment, then, is a life force, a consistency with the self at its deepest levels, an encounter with God and grace in all their compelling passion. It is interwoven with integrity and unfearful of intimacy.

Commitment is, therefore, more demanding and enriching than life–long concurrence with an earlier word one may have pledged. This word may not have been profound enough when it was first spoken. Or, if it were indeed at that time, it may have to be put aside now because even more is asked of us. Jephthah's word was deep and serious when he formulated his vow but his daughter's life introduced a more substantive reality into his life, one he refused to be faithful to because he was blinded by fidelity to his earlier word.

Everyone knows a committed person when one sees him or her. No institution need point out such a person. Life knows life and remains life even though some institutions choose to define it differently.

THREE QUESTIONS

Implicit in this question of vows and solemn promises are issues of over–riding significance. My attitude to my former word and commitment is influenced by my evaluation of other realities in my life. I would like to isolate three of the more salient concerns.

1. Who is God and how does God deal with us?

Is God, we might ask ourselves, someone who is revealed only in someone else's life? Or, is God someone who is revealed in my own life? God, I believe, tells me who God is, not only in the community of the Church and of the world but also in the context of my own life. When, therefore, I make decisions and choices from the deepest levels of my being, when I elect, for example, to marry, with all the passion and conviction, with all the suffering and ecstasy that election presupposes, especially for a priest, is God part of that in no way? When I choose to dispose of my life in such a radical manner, could God truly be a stranger to me? Is God part of that decision in no way, a decision in which my whole future and my very identity are at stake? If not, what kind of a God do I believe in and worship? If I feel that God has not blessed me in my marriage as well as in my priesthood, if I feel that God was with me in celibacy but not in sexual commitment, then what kind of a God do I profess to love?

As far as I can understand God's plan for the human family, marriage is at the core and center of it. It is the first blessing God gives to human life. It is also the first instance in the chronology of Jesus whose life begins with the marital commitment of Mary and Joseph.

In the plan of God, marriage is first. Priesthood comes about much later in the history of revelation. Celibacy is the last of these gifts. All these developments are good but marriage is the first blessing, the only blessing of the three (marriage, priesthood, celibacy) which is essential for the survival of the human family and, of course, the Church.

Is it not possible that God called us to marriage after priesthood because God had confidence in us? Are our marriages to be prophetic statements, challenging the Church to reconsider its order of priorities? At this moment of history, the marriages we entered into would demand of us far more courage and sacrifice than those marriages will in the future. These marriages required of us a profound poverty, the poverty of setting aside clerical privileges and conveniences, indeed key aspects of our identity and meaning. Such marriages make substantive contributions, I believe, to the reform of the Church and the renewal of people's lives.

And, so, we have been called. It was always that way with us, was it not? We must give God back in gratitude more than guilt and insecurity, more than resentment and anger at the Church whose life we are serving in a special fashion, more than indifference and apathy in the vocation for which God has elected us in an altogether unique manner.

If a vow or promise of celibacy had been held to rigidly, all of this would have been lost.

2. What is the Church and how are we part of it?

If truth be told, many of us were more committed to clerical culture than we imagined. Obligatory celibacy reinforced this attachment. We grieve, at times, over our loss of clerical identity more than we do over our priesthood (which is enduring) or over our place in the Church (which is indelibly ours).

Indeed, it may well be that we valued the laity as such and women in particular less than we do now. We once assumed, did we not, that ordination was a more important sacrament than baptism, that is was more vital for the Church's life. This assumption is, of course, unbiblical, untraditional, untheological, non–pastoral in its implications.

In a survey done for the National Conference of Catholic Bishops, fifty–six percent of resigned priests still consider themselves priests; almost eight out of ten (78%) consider themselves Catholic. What has been lost, then, is clerical identity and some aspects of ministry, many of which may be continued if we choose. In a further study about resigned priests (1982), canonical priests gave overwhelming positive ratings to the ministry once exercised by their married priests brothers.

By every standard of measurement, it is clear that the hour for a married priesthood has come. Scripture calls for it as does the tradition of the Church. Indeed, we are not asking for an innovation but for a restoration, the restoration of a married priesthood which has been an option for most of Church history. Pastoral life requires such a priesthood and the signs of the time denote its urgency and its inevitability. Collegiality, women's rights and ecumenism will not make significant progress while obligatory celibacy is maintained. Liberation theology and the base community movement seek a married priesthood. The desire for a married priesthood has been expressed in overwhelming majorities by women as well as men, by clergy as well as laity, by religious as well as diocesan priests, by old as well as young, by the entire world, in every country, on every level of economic and social life. The time has come.

What kind of a Church insists on obligatory celibacy in the face of all this? A Church which has no future. The Church of Jephthah is dying; the Church of God's Spirit is taking its place. It is the Church of Jephthah which hides in fear, refusing to allow this issue to be discussed by the pastoral leaders of the Church, punishing those who declare publicly what is present in the hearts of God's People, refusing to promote priests or bishops who plead for a Church which recognizes fully all the ministries to which women and married Catholics are called by God.

The call for a married priesthood challenges the idolatry and absoluteness of the Church, the authoritarianism and vengeful spirit which are unworthy of it. The more happy we are as married priests, the more public we are about our vocation, the less bitter and angry we are, the less we become victims of guilt or insecurity, the more able we are to see our role as prophetic and charismatic, then the more thoroughly we become a sign of that future Church God's People yearn for with an intensity which is painful in its ardor and in its need.

Obligatory celibacy was once a policy the Church endorsed many centuries ago against the worldliness of the Church, its involvement in money and property, power and privilege. It has now become a sign of the worldly Church, one which closes its heart and its ears and chooses instead an arsenal of weapons against its own people: censorship and threats; punishment and sacramental deprivation: dismissals and condemnations.

All this will not work, because the Church is more than that. It will not work because we, our families and our friends, are not worthy of such treatment and the Church at large knows this. All the indecency of this aspect of the Church's life will come to nought through the quiet love with which we embrace our wives and children and, yes, the Church itself. In contemplative tranquillity we shall go on trusting that God will not abandon God's own People and that Christ will be present as he always is when love is authentic, sacrificial, and faithful. John XXIII once observed that the Church has no enemies even though some may hate it. The Church of Christ must not consider as enemies those ordained Christians who come to it in love and offer their lives in service.

Thomas Merton said it well:
"What is a Church, after all, but a community in which truth is shared, not a monopoly that dispenses it from the top down?" (*Hidden Ground of Love*)

3. Who am I and what is human life all about?

We need to ask ourselves whether we believe that our lives are greater than our commitments. If our life serves our commitments, then we are closer once again to the God of Jephthah. Commitment is not the source of our identity but only a product of it.

Who am I? I am a human being, made by God for relationship and love, first of all, and for service and happiness. Any commitments I make along the way need to be affirmed within this context. Commitment must create love or else it dishonors God and misrepresents God's commitment to us in making us. Commitment is to be maintained with relative ease, not harshly and brutally, so that all our energy goes into the commitment and little is left for service and life.

We have been made for joy and ecstasy. Is this not what we teach our children? We have been made for passion and celebration, for beauty and peace. Have we taught our children they were made only for discipline and sacrifice? Of course we have not. Then why have we not understood this better ourselves?

When I remember my parents, the most precious memories I have of them from my childhood were the times they played with me. Why? Because play and leisure is what is deepest about us. Our God is God of the dance, a poet who made, in the beginning, a paradise and a special relationship between the first man and the first woman.

The Christian community is most enchanted by the Jesus of Christmas and Easter, events when Jesus was not constrained but somehow sovereignly free. The cross and the darkness are real moments in the life of Jesus but they are interludes. Jesus dies no more; he is forever Easter; and we are his People.

My evaluation of the promise I once made to be celibate tells me a great deal about who God is for me and what I believe of the Church. It is a statement about how I value my own life and what I think of the place of love in it. My attitude toward my earlier word lets me know how much I value freedom and love, and the price I will pay for them.

COMMITMENT AS TERROR AND COMMITMENT AS FIDELITY

Loyalty, it seems to me, is a two-way street. We must be loyal to the Church but the Church must be faithful to us. Some policies in the Church deserve no fidelity. To serve them is to dishonor the Church and to deny the vocation we have been given.

If the Church cannot find an adequate place for married priests, it becomes, at least to this extent, an anti-life Church. What can be a more compelling sign of life than marriage and children? A Church which forbids such life to its priests, a Church which rejects the call of God's People for a married priesthood, is a Church which acts against life and justice, indeed, against its own interests and its own people. Any policy which must be maintained with terror and dishonesty creates a heart of darkness in the Body of the Church, a spirit which Christ resists with all his love.

The Church is only true to itself when it says that it needs no weapons and it fears none of its children. The Church is most itself when it is a faithful lover, when it calls us to discipline but not as its first order of preference, when it speaks to us of life, sometimes painfully, but not when it silences all the alternative voices of its own sons and daughters.

A study done for the National Conference of Catholic Bishops states that the main problem in the Church cited by resigned priests is the abuse of authority. Those in canonical priesthood list the way authority is exercised as the most serious of some fifteen personal problems they encounter in their priesthood.

The abuse of authority creates a docile clergy but one which becomes so oblique to people's lives, so marginal to the Church's real needs that few young people want to follow such a calling. And so, our seminaries become bare, ruined choirs and priests who once dreamed, at their ordination, of a renewed world and a reformed church and a spirit–filled priesthood settle into complacency, into the terror which resides at the heart of an institution which has come to mistrust everything it does not approve and allow.

At the core of the Church's life, there is an awareness that its present abuse of authority is wrong. And, so, married priests function in the Eastern Catholic Churches and, now, in the Latin Rite, provided that no promise of celibacy has been made at any point in a person's life.

This promise, once made, achieves an autonomy of its own, one which is seen as central, one which makes peripheral all previous and all subsequent decisions and choices. The only reason why a married priest is punished and forbidden to function fully is because of a promise of celibacy, one which means more than marriage or priesthood, children or faith, pastoral needs or truth, grace or love. Celibacy has become, at this point, neither life–style nor gift but taboo.

There is a tendency for some in the Church to equate the promise of celibacy with the vow of marriage and to compare optional celibacy with divorce. Even the official Church does not go this far. It grants no divorces, at least not divorces it is willing to call such. It does grant dispensations from celibacy, a dispensation which says, in effect, that both parties declare the promise or vow non–existent. If both parties who made the agreement agree it is no longer binding, why are we punished? Is it not legitimate to conclude that such a promise is not even a broken promise, merely, a non–existent one? Why, then, are we punished? If the promise is broken, then the Church has been a party in breaking it. Why then are we punished and God's People with us? Would any of us release a child from a promise and then punish the child?

The Church can dispense as it chooses from obligatory celibacy because it knows such celibacy has not come from God directly but has always been an institutional policy. Why then does the institution punish itself by seeking to terminate the ministry and priesthood of some 100,000 married priests? Why must the laity be burdened with the lack of adequate pastoral leadership? We ask again and again but there are no answers. Only, the response: "It is the law. It is our will." Where is Christ's Spirit in all this?

The demise of celibacy in the Catholic community has not come about because people are less able to maintain celibacy or less generous in their love for God and for people. The demise of celibacy has come about because people no longer believe in it as institutional policy. They have found other ways to be faithful and sacrificial, sometimes far better ways to be creative and committed. Many currently celibate priests know they will be better priests if they are married. They remain celibate not because they believe Christ wishes this or the priesthood requires it but because one man, the Pope, has decided they must live this way. The Pope's decision is oppressive when it can only be maintained by threat and power. The Pope is more than that, is he not? We hope in him to settle this issue and bring peace to the Church. Every effort, except optional celibacy, has been used to resolve the crisis. None has worked. None will work. The answer to the crisis in pastoral leadership is essentially bound up with the restoration of a married priesthood.

CONCLUSION

My brothers, when you and I offered ourselves for ordination, it was with the priesthood in mind as our central commitment. Had there been only a married priesthood allowable, we would have sought priesthood after marriage. There was, instead, only obligatory celibacy and so we sought priesthood in that context.

Let us, however, be honest about this. We did accept celibacy, as a commitment and in freedom. This celibacy was, for many of us, a creative experience. Indeed, the growth we were gifted with, from celibacy, may explain the extraordinary happiness the vast majority of married priests find in marriage. In this sense, we have brought our celibacy and our priesthood into our marriages.

Let us be honest also in saying that we had no intention then or now that celibacy should control our priesthood and become essential to its exercise. How did a condition for ordination become the very substance of our commitment? Would any of us, were we to make the decision, ordain a candidate for whom priestly ministry was incidental to celibacy?

Let us be honest once again about the fact that it was the priesthood and the unique ministry which went with it which captured our hearts and our spirits. Our memories do not cluster around documents we signed about celibate commitments but around ordination day and the Eucharist. We remember the blessings we gave and received, the anointing of our hands and hearts, the love we had for a God who could bring us, in all our unworthiness, to such a commitment, to such a grace.

In any case, we are here, my bothers. And we are here in many cases, with our wives and children. We have given ourselves to a new fidelity, one which assumes and absorbs all our priesthood and the substance of our life in the arms of our wives and in the hearts of our children. We are still faithful but to a different Church, a new Church, one which all God's People need us to help them build. We are the bridge between the old and the new since we have lived in both Churches, between clerical and lay life since we have known both profoundly, between celibacy and marriage since we have been given both gifts.

We must not cease our efforts or ever doubt that words and ideas are powerful realities in our lives. Lenin once said: "Ideas are much more fatal than guns." Ideas are decisive. The ideas and words of a new Church are alive in every man, woman and child here. Every word we speak, all the words of this meeting change the world in some way. Didn't Jesus teach us about the value of the word? Even Lenin knew that. We must renew our confidence in our words and ideas. We are wedded to the new Church by the witness of God's Spirit and by the words of fidelity we speak at this meeting.

We shall prevail if we can only believe it is God's Word and God's Work which is being done in us. We must believe with all our hearts that God has made us saints, not because we are good but because God has called us to make the Church holy. We once thought God's holiness was in us when we were ordained and anointed, uplifted for God's People and blessed by their love. Do we think this is all over? When God has sworn, God does not repent. Remember those words? Do we suppose we are saints no longer? Who told us we were not? Why did we believe them?

Where was our sanctity lost? Did we lose sanctity in the arms of our wives? We found grace there and we were blessed by our wives. Did we lose sanctity in the children we conceived and held in our arms, willing to die for them if need be? We found God in our children, in their hearts, and they blessed us. Did we lose sanctity because we asked God to be with us as we took our word of celibacy and made it a vow of marriage? We were given two sacraments at that moment and summoned to be doubly committed, to marriage and to priesthood until death. Mysteriously, both sacraments became one lived reality in us so that all the commitments became of marriage and priesthood became one life. In our wives and children, Christ was formed for us as he became bone of our bone, flesh of our flesh. What God put together in us, let no mortal power put asunder.

Jesus once said: "If you love me, I will come to you and you will be my disciples." Words of such heart–breaking tenderness can never cease to echo in our lives. We must hear them as we age and die, as we love and prevail.

My brothers and my sisters, your marriages brought love into the world, a love which would have withered and died had you turned away from it and not been faithful to each other. You brought children into the Church and taught them of Christ. You brought peace and joy and freedom into this sometimes bleak and broken century. Nothing was ever broken in you, certainly not the promise of your life.

Would God ever take God's own Word out of us because we loved and gave life? What kind of a God would that be?

Where is the shape of the future priesthood and the life of the new

Church? It is here. It is in every choice we ever made for Love over the Law. It is in every memory we nurture of that new commandment of Love which broke the rigidity of Jephthah's God and the heartlessness of Jephthah's vow. Our God takes no one away from love.

Where is the shape of the future priesthood? It is here. It is ourselves, all unworthy though we be. For, you see, it was God who made us priests. God has sworn. It was God who called us to marriage. God does not repent.

Let us make no mistake in this regard. The stakes are too high, the price too costly. Marriage for us was priesthood on another level, consecration in a new form, commitment in its most concrete and inescapable expression.

We, all of us, have served God less well than God deserved but we have loved God more ardently than we imagined.

"If you love me, I will come to you and you will be my disciples." Do we not remember? How could we forget? Would God ever take away our priesthood because we loved our wives? What kind of a God would that be?

15

GALILEO'S TELESCOPE

It is not healthy to live and work in one world and to believe and pray in another. The harmony of these two worlds is an issue in the development of a contemporary spirituality.

TWO MILLENNIA AND FIVE CENTURIES

Gospel, Church and world are three pivotal points in the Church's life over its first two millennia. The Gospel dominates the first five centuries as the canon of Scripture, the creeds and Christology are formulated. The sixth to the fifteenth centuries are engaged with the Church, its structure, councils, sacraments, judicial system and religious institutions. The last five centuries are concerned with the autonomy of the world and the discovery of its own sacred character. Let us focus on this latter period, an epoch beginning with the discovery of the new world in 1492 and leading to the birth of the new Europe some 500 years later. The task of the twenty–first century, I believe, will be an integration of Gospel, Church and World. The present crisis in the Church derives from the lack of synthesis. Each of these last five centuries might be illustrated by choosing a person or event to represent it.

THE BEGINNING: COLUMBUS(1492)

Columbus overcame the limited vision of the planet by finding, within the very world he thought he knew, a new world. This led

Europe and the Church to redefine their sense of the planet's center and it revealed that there was more to the world than they supposed. The world after Columbus was more difficult for the Church to control. It manifested its integrity independently of the Church's sense of it.

The new world resisted defining itself in terms of monarchy; it saw the secular order as valuable in its own right, separated Church and State, inaugurated national democracies, fused together ethnic, racial and religious groups, and generated pragmatic as well as liberation theologies. The world was forever different after Columbus and more autonomous than it was before him.

THE SIXTEENTH CENTURY: LUTHER

If Columbus redesigned the world in the fifteenth century, Luther redefined the Church in the sixteenth century. Columbus helped us to see that the center of the world was not where people supposed it was. Luther shifted the center of the Church from the papacy to the New Testament, from the hierarchy to people, from sacraments to conscience, from authority to consensus. Luther called for a new relationship with the world, one which saw marriage as a good in itself and not as a concession to human weakness, one which expanded the notion of vocation to include not only clerical callings but worldly tasks. To be a lay person in Luther's Church was to exist in a fully privileged state of life, not inferior to ordained pastors; a lay person could be wholeheartedly a citizen of the world and need not go to a monastery or join the clergy to enhance one's relationship with God. The world was different after Columbus; it began to be seen as sacred after Luther.

THE SEVENTEENTH CENTURY: GALILEO

It was especially with Galileo that the world took on a different significance. Galileo somehow makes the world both sacred and insignificant. It is sacred because it is addressed in its own terms. It is insignificant because the world is no longer the stationary center of the solar system. Galileo does not yet have the key of how to endow the world with significance again. Einstein will show us that the relationship of the insignificant to everything else in the cosmos is what makes it significant.

"Truth," Galileo declares in Bertolt Brecht's play, "is the daughter of Time, not of Authority." Authority, we might observe, adds nothing to Truth; it is Truth which gives moral force to Authority. Truth is larger than the Church. The Church only proclaims the Truth effectively if it learns first how to serve the Truth. In the case of Galileo, the Church demands that the Truth be judged in the Church's terms, as though the Truth were smaller than the Church.

The drama between Galileo and the Inquisition is heightened by the tension between the validity of human experience and the demands of those who dismiss data which displease them.

Brecht's play, *Galileo,* reminds us "You can't make a man unsee what he has seen."

Galileo, unfortunately, gives in to the Inquisition. He consoles himself with the thought that "There is not such thing as a scientific work only one man can write." When his disappointed colleagues speak of how sad a land is when it has no heroes, Galileo replies: "Unhappy is the land that needs a hero."

A Church that requires one man to write its theology and set its policies, a Church which needs only one man to be a hero in it, is an unhappy Church. If theology is Truth, then anyone can write it. The Truth is compelling in its own right; it does not have to be obligatory. If the Church is a healthy community, then it needs no hero; its own life is the heroic deed and all its members are the heroic gesture. A family does not need a hero; it needs love and forgiveness and relationship so that all its members come to believe they are valued.

Galileo once asked a persistent critic of his, Giulio Libri, a philosopher at the University of Pisa, to come to Florence and look through the telescope. Libri replied that there was no need to do so because he knew the Truth already.

In 1600, Rome burned to death the Dominican Friar Giordano Bruno for teaching that the earth moves. Ten years later, Galileo published the same thesis and proved with his telescope that the world was different from the Church's definition of it. In 1633, Galileo, threatened with torture and death, capitulated to the Inquisition. He remained a prisoner, despite his recantation, until his death in 1642.

All the world knows this: it was not Galileo Rome imprisoned but a Truth it could not control and could not make less than itself.

It has been said that Galileo shouted out in moral triumph "Eppur si muove." The earth moves and Rome cannot stop it. It moves because the world is sacred, with its own integrity and meaning, regardless of what Rome says of it. The Truth is not made in Rome. Before the Truth, Rome is a servant, the servant of the servants of God.

Rome can no longer be the immovable center of an ecclesiastical solar system. It cannot sit in judgment of Columbus and Luther and Galileo; it must relate to them and move with them and learn from them and correct its errors and become a mobile part rather than the immutable center of reality.

The Truth cannot be arrested in its forward movement or confined in the prison of lesser worlds.

THE EIGHTEENTH CENTURY: THE AMERICAN REVOLUTION

As one moves into the Eighteenth Century, one must become delicate with one's choices. The sacredness and autonomy of the world are accelerating. The world's value is proclaimed not only by Galileo but also by the Renaissance and the Enlightenment, not only by the American Revolution but also by the French Revolution. The Truth is seen as something which abides in the world as it does in the Church, in the minds of human beings as easily, as readily, as it does in the magisterium, in the texture of everyday life as surely as it does in the texts of Scripture. When modern people wish to have their experience validated or the Truth tested, they go, not to the Church first, but to the world.

Truth is now clearly seen as the daughter of Time rather than of Authority. It is not the work of one person, even a Pope, or of one institution, even the Church, but the collaborative and collegial work of the entire human family.

The Truth, like the Risen Christ, is not obliged to reveal itself in the Temple or even in the priesthood. Like the Risen Christ, the Truth may appear anywhere. It is not the task of the beholder to predict or to control the appearance but to recognize its validity. The disciples had no Authority to proclaim Easter and needed none. They were convincing because they themselves were convinced; it was what they saw and experienced which they proclaimed; they too were imprisoned by a religious system for their convictions. They did not fear open debate or disagreement but religious leaders of their time did.

As one enters the Eighteenth Century, the work of Columbus, Luther and Galileo are seen to be essentially correct. Perhaps I might be forgiven the choice of the American Revolution as the representative event for this century. I make this choice partly because I am an American, more substantially because it succeeded, I would argue, in keeping Church and world in friendly alliance even though the Revolution made the Church and world separate, liberating the world from a need to be defined by the Church.

In any case, allow me to say that the American Revolution was a strong protest, not against a Europe-centered world (which Columbus shattered) nor against an oppressive papal center for the Church (which Luther shattered) nor against an earth-centered cosmos (which Galileo shattered) but against a monarch-centered nation (which the American Revolution shattered).

The American Revolution returns the nation to people just as Luther returned the Church to the laity. Like Columbus, it had no maps to this new world of national democracy and constitutional limits. It built its new structures from observation and experiment, as Galileo did, and it defined the Truth in its own integrity without seeking the Church's endorsement. Legitimacy would come not from the Church but from the electorate, now seen capable of validating the Truth from the work of the Spirit, if you will, in its midst. America trusted people as Luther once trusted the laity.

If Columbus changed the geography of the world and Luther the definition of the Church and Galileo the boundaries of the solar system, the American Revolution changed the constitution of the political order in the modern world. The Bill of Rights declares the autonomy and sacredness of the human person; checks and balances restrict the ability of one minister of government to define Truth as the daughter of its own authority.

In all of this, I do not wish to give America more than its due nor do I suggest that there was not a dark side to the American Revolution and its aftermath. Nonetheless, the world is profoundly different and autonomous after the American Revolution as it was after Columbus, Luther and Galileo.

THE NINETEENTH CENTURY: DARWIN

My choice of Darwin is not done without competitors. Marx and Freud are also candidates. I choose Darwin because the work of Marx and Freud may be less clearly correct in as many of its parts. In any case, this is not a comprehensive paper nor one immune to challenge and improvement. It is my intent to discern patterns and dynamics rather than to achieve universal agreement or to exclude alternative possibilities.

Darwin's thought will be condemned by the Church as was the American separation of Church and State. Eppur si muove. The Truth goes on even when Authority calls a halt to its march through time. Since Truth is not Authority's daughter, Authority has no parental rights or moral influence over it.

In Darwin, human biology is freed to pursue its own autonomy or Truth since it has not been set rigidly by God but formed, almost capriciously, by Time. The Church's ability to base its ethics on the absoluteness of human biology is dealt a severe blow by Darwin. The Church will reject the data once again without examination and will declare in the twentieth century that human biology, seen as absolute and unchangeable, predetermines the ethical judgment on contraception and abortion, artificial insemination, in vitro fertilization, and the right to die. All of these realities are supposedly resolved by the priority of human biology over human choice, indeed by making human biology the immovable center of an ethical solar system, if you will. Once again, the Church declares it has no need to look through the telescope. All of these issues, Rome declares, are settled in advance and without exception. Indeed, the sovereignty of human biology is invoked to define the ethics of homosexuality and even to dictate whether women may be ordained to the priesthood. I am not saying that Rome is incorrect in all these instances, though it may well be, but I am suggesting that Rome is working again with the wrong solar system.

In the nineteenth century, Church representatives declared that human biology was not developed from lower forms of life, that it existed in splendid isolation from them and that the Church knew this with certainty. In a previous century, the Church had declared that the earth was the center of the solar system and that it knew this with certainty.

One is astonished, in the light of how often the Church was simply wrong in the modern era, at its audacity in proclaiming papal infallibility. It could only do this effectively under a Pope, Pius IX, who rejected the entire modern world and its political order as evil and who sought to control the Truth in a papal center. Pius IX did this in the *Syllabus of Errors* before calling the First Vatican Council to define his infallibility.

THE TWENTIETH CENTURY: EINSTEIN

With Einstein, we come to understand that the universe has no center and that interrelationship is what holds the whole of reality together.

It has been said that we pattern our lives on the models of the universe our culture gives us. There have been three models during the two millennia of the Church's existence.

The first of these was the Ptolemaic model. It envisioned the universe as an earth-centered reality and arranged the spheres or planets around it in a strict hierarchical order. The empyrean, or the stars, for example, were seen as pure and everlasting; the earth was dark and mortal. We find this model in Dante's *Divina Commedia.*

This model prevailed through the ten centuries, the fifth to the fifteenth, when the structure of the hierarchical Church was put in place. The Pope and Bishops existed in splendid isolation from the rest of the Church; they had direct communication with God and were sacred personages in a way the laity, unless they were royal, were not. This Ptolemaic universe gave us a Ptolemaic Papacy.

The second of these models was the Newtonian model. It was developed after Galileo by Isaac Newton. It is a heliocentered system dominated not by hierarchical spheres but by absolute clarity and translucent mathematical laws. All is in movement but nothing is in doubt; everything is mechanistically determined in a clock-work, impersonal universe. This model prevails during the sixteenth to the twentieth centuries.

These centuries give us what I would call a Newtonian Magisterium. The Church now accelerates the development of a teaching authority in which everything can be settled, clarified and resolved in the Church's terms. There is to be one model theology for the Church, one form of worship, one canon law, one approved catechism, one celibate priesthood. The Newtonian Magisterium eventually declares itself infallible. The question raised now in the Church, especially among the Bishops, is not whether what the Pope says is true or even useful but whether the Pope has decided to teach infallibly or not. Certitude and clarity are seen as primary values; doubt and ambiguity are considered weaknesses. When Paul VI issues *Humanae Vitae* which is, after all, only an encyclical and not a Council, the question raised anxiously in the Church was whether this teaching was infallible or not, clear and final for all time or whether Catholics were permitted to discuss it. John Paul II appoints bishops whose teaching on all matters of Church doctrine and discipline is to be unambiguously clear. The Newtonian Magisterium is certain, unbending, mechanistic, impersonal, and unreachable. Truth is no longer the daughter of Time but of Authority.

Einstein gives us a third model, a universe relative and relational in all its parts, participatory in every instance. Every atom influences every other so that nothing exists in isolation. There is no hierarchy; the universe is catholic and universal. There is no clarity; the universe is a profound mystery and we stand in awe before it.

The only Ecumenical Council held since Einstein, Vatican II, is a Council which reflects this. It calls for collegiality and community, declares none of its teaching infallible and gives us participatory images of the Church as the People of God and the Liturgy as the work of the priesthood of all believers. It tells us the Church is a mystery and calls for a community of local Churches with different cultures, theologies and traditions. Vatican II is vastly different from the Ptolemaic Papacy of an Innocent III for example. It does not require, as Vatican I did, Newtonian clarity, papal infallibility and rational certitude to make its point.

In Einstein's universe, all is in movement and nothing is at rest. If movement could stop for an instant, the universe would end. "I move, therefore, I am," one might say.

It is foolish in such a context to continue obligatory celibacy only because we have done this for a long time or to reaffirm the prohibition of contraception because change might confuse people. It is unconvincing to deny the ordination of women because we have not ordained women in the past.

Change, in Einstein's universe, is not frantic but creative; all is held in check by its relationship to everything else. Einstein tells us that the universe has a shape but no center and that no part gives direction and purpose to all the other parts.

By theological application, we might maintain that God does not exist in any center but is somehow everywhere. There is no privileged place to be; it is a privilege just to be. And God is fully there. All parts of the body are fully alive, no one part more alive than any other. Indeed, it is the whole body which is alive as all its parts come together so that the body is somehow less a body when a part is missing.

Einstein put the separate pieces of the universe together and showed how they relate to one another. He joined light to time and time to space and space to gravity and energy to matter. As he did this, he could not know that he was giving us the dynamics which would lead to Vatican II. John XXIII opened a window and looked through Galileo's telescope and called a Council. And so, now, we seek to join the papacy to the bishops and bishops to people and priests to community and authority to conscience and sacred to secular and Gospel to World and Christianity to other religions and Catholicism to Orthodoxy and Protestantism and male to female and America to Europe and Socialism to Capitalism and stability to change and marriage to priesthood.

Our voyage is to a new world, sometimes without maps but never without one another, always with a measure of fear but not without hope, able to recognize a new continent in the pale October moonlight of 1492 or a new Church in the open window of October 1962, when Vatican II begins. Our voyage is through the broken Berlin Wall and beyond Tienanman Square and it enlists the free hearts of former Soviet citizens and the free spirit which now brings all of Europe together. Our companions on this journey are the people we love and the children we bear, the dreams we fashion in darkness and the prayers we formulate at dawn, the commitments we choose and the love we make and the tears we shed and the songs we sing.

Only a static Church in a changing universe could deny all this life or seek to punish it. Had that Church had its way Luther and Galileo and democracy and evolution would all have perished. This static Church would prefer that we look to the infallible papacy to settle all questions about the Church and the solar system, about the priesthood of all believers and the origin of the species, about the separation of

Church and State and even the issues we may publicly debate. In a universe of infinite majesty and movement, a Ptolemaic Papacy and a Newtonian Magisterium are quaint and inert.

JOHN'S WINDOW

Cardinal Barberini was a friend of Galileo and receptive to Galileo's ideas. When he became Pope Urban VIII, however, he threatened Galileo with torture until he recanted and denied the validity of his data. How could Urban VIII have done this to a friend whose theories, he realized, were persuasive?

In his play, *Galileo*, Bertolt Brecht gives us a plausible solution. Brecht portrays Urban VIII discussing the Galileo case with the Cardinal Inquisitor. During their conversation, the Pope attires for a ceremony. Before he vests, he is open to Galileo. As each vestment is put on him, he becomes more hostile. When he is fully vested, he finds torture acceptable.

Brecht shows us a Pope who lives and works in one world, who believes and prays in another. Urban VIII denies the validity of his own experience for the demands of an institution and his own position in it. Truth is the casualty in this denial of evidence. Galileo and Urban VIII are separated by the papacy and by their choice to live in two different solar systems. In Galileo's system, truth is not discovered by authority but in time; human experience, the world's autonomy, intellectual concerns are seen as convincing. In Urban's system, truth is made by authority; human experience, the world and the intellect are discarded. This tension between two solar systems, so to speak, is at the heart of the crisis of the Church.

In our lifetime, a very different Pope, John XXIII, opened a window and the Second Vatican Council in 1962. He declared in the inaugural speech at the Council that "violence inflicted on others" gives us "no help at all in finding a happy solution to our problems." The Second Vatican in *Gaudium et Spes* described the world as meaningful in its own right; it saw marriage as a relationship of life and love and it discovered God in the signs of the times.

Out of these correlations and connections an utterly new spirituality will be generated, one which derives as much from the world as it does from the Gospel, as much from the personality of each person as it does from the Church and its tradition. As believers move into this new universe, they will discover that it has no center; the center will be created where life happens intensely and where it maintains a relationship with other life.

This spirituality will not develop from general principles enunciated by a universal Church in some theoretical manner but from those passionate experiences which move the human heart profoundly and take it beyond itself. It is only when we feel our humanity move to its depths, to its point of exhaustion and transcendence, that we begin to know who Christ was and what Incarnation is. It is passion which breaks the human heart open so that God can enter. Doctrine and theology, sacral institutions and legal systems, as such, do not do this, especially when they alienate us from our identities and compel us to live in a world whose center and solar systems are artificial and contrived. The reason why so much Church teaching is irrelevant is because it is written for a world which does not exist anymore and is addressed to lives which have not yet found their own center.

It is noteworthy that the disciples in the Gospels do not find Jesus in the Temple. They discover Jesus as they work in the open fields and on turbulent seas. They encounter Jesus where they experience life. In the Pastoral Epistles we are instructed to choose our Church leaders only from those who have made a passionate commitment to one woman and who have entered deeply into family life. The early Church was a domestic Church and its ritual was the celebration of a family meal. It did not need the Temple to make it holy. Its sanctity came from the memories and hopes one brought to the meal, from the love and passion with which life was shared, and from the spirit of God which became present to all this. The early Church needed little structure to sustain it; wherever two or three gathered, the Church became possible and Christ was present. We must not, of course, romanticize this early Church so that we see it as having no problems. We cite it only because its priorities seem to have been better than ours.

In this early assembly of Christians, Peter was still a fisherman and Paul a tent maker; apostles had families and the gathering of the community made the Eucharist happen. It was important to know the faces and names around the table because the Eucharist did not depend upon the priesthood, even less upon celibacy, but upon the memories, hopes, passions and lives of those who gathered.

When Einstein gave us a limitless model for the universe and when John XXIII opened a window, our hearts and souls were exposed to all the agony and ecstasy of our concrete lives. Confusion may follow as we enter this new world and restructure our lives so that they fit our times. We may indeed experience a dark night of the soul. The dark night of the soul is the act by which we fall from a lesser truth to a greater truth. The greater truth is a unified world in which we can live and work and pray and believe. We can no longer return to a world which subjects Truth to obedience or passion to an institution or conscience to law. We wish no more to do this now than the disciples of Jesus wished to become Temple priests. They preferred to break bread in the open fields and in the warmth of their own homes and families. We have learned well what the early disciples knew, namely, that the human heart and the real world must not be denied since God abides preeminently in them.

CODA

As we complete these reflections, let us keep in mind the images which unified them: Columbus' flagship and Luther's ninety-five theses, Galileo's telescope and the American Bill of Rights, Darwin's organic connections and Einstein's open-ended equations. All of these images were formed in passion and vibrated with life so abundant that it could not be contained in the old wineskins of lesser truths and visions.

Nothing less than God and Truth are at issue in all this. The universe and the new Church bring with them the new Christ who bursts open the confinements of lesser worlds and restrictive Church systems. The Risen Christ is less clearly defined than the historical Jesus but we feel this Christ more passionately in our hearts. The first disciples did not find the Risen Christ in the Temple. He came to them as they worked on the seas again and when they gathered as a family in the Upper Room. The New Christian Church seemed worldly to the traditional Jewish establishment. It appeared outrageous as it extended the priesthood to all believers.

But the spirit compelled the disciples ever forward, into the whole world, beyond Jerusalem, into a limitless universe. There they found their mission.

16

Joseph's Son

While teaching at the University of Notre Dame, I joined some faculty for dinner one evening. A noted Scripture scholar sat next to me. In the course of conversation, I asked my colleague what he thought of the question whether Jesus ever married.

His reaction, delivered in three sharp sentences, was swift.

The question is silly, a waste of time. To even raise the question is to lose academic respectability. Only approved and respected authors should be followed in these matters. As I worked through these comments, I was left with the distinct impression he did not wish to continue the conversation.

The response of this respected, intelligent, inquisitive, on occasion even courageous scholar was astonishing. He never asked why I raised the question and never inquired about the evidence. He was uncomfortable with the issue and would not tolerate any discussion of it.

The reaction was more typical than I would have suspected before I began research on this topic.

A theologian, William Phipps, who had wondered about whether Jesus was married recorded some of the letters he received.

1. Had Jesus been married, he would have been crucified not once but twice. (No record is available about whether a man or woman wrote this letter.)

2. The important work Jesus did for God kept him from wasting his time on a woman. (I suspect it was a man who wrote that letter.)

3. More typical was this response: Jesus could not have been married

because he did not do shameful things. (This letter speaks for itself and is too sad in its implications for further comment.)

4. A married Jesus would be lower than the angels and just like us. (The writer seems to be ashamed both of the Incarnation and of humanity in general.)

5. And, finally; Jesus had no navel and, therefore, would be incapable of sex. (I am still working on this one and would appreciate any help I can get in understanding it. I have the distinct impression that some of us may be missing out on something in marriage. I stand in awe at the power of the human imagination and the endless variety of sexual possibilities.)

Allow me to return from navel gazing to Notre Dame. A few of us remained in conversation after my Scripture colleague left the table. Another faculty member inquired about why I had asked the question.

Since I am a married priest some may suspect that my research is driven by a personal agenda. If, however, we question whether a married priest is objective in discussing the marriage of Jesus we must also wonder about the objectivity of a celibate priest in considering the celibacy of Jesus.

Whether the writer is married or celibate should be of no concern. Let the evidence offered speak for itself.

In any case, the question I raise is a question. We shall, perhaps, never have certitude on the marriage or celibacy of Jesus. Although I believe the evidence suggests a probability Jesus was married, I can also see values in a celibate Jesus. Each celibate is called to make a decision that, granting the unique circumstances of his or her life, and taking into account the work one is doing and the values one is pursuing, celibacy is the better option. It would be a tragedy if we used subtle or overt pressure to assure that all were married.

It is quite possible that Jesus was always celibate and that his celibacy became a witness against what was essentially mandatory marriage in Judaism. If this were the case, however, it is both strange and unfortunate that neither Jesus nor the New Testament present this option clearly.

We need to be attentive to the magnitude and mystery of Jesus' personality and not reduce Jesus to the logical, conventional or cultural requirements of his age.

There is always the danger that the researcher may tailor the facts to fit the theory or that the prevailing notions and norms of one's own day might be read back into history as a way of making Jesus understandable in our terms.

Before Jesus, we stand into awe, whatever our conclusion or personal assumptions.

THE ASSUMPTIONS WE MAKE

As I began research on this issue, I reflected on the assumptions I had made in the past on a number of questions.

The Second Vatican Council opened in October, 1962. I was a seminary professor at the time with a doctorate in theology from Rome and a graduate degree in philosophy. I mention the credentials so that we can measure more readily the culpability of my ignorance.

Had a seminarian asked me whether the Church could ordain women as priests, I would have assumed that there was adequate biblical evidence and impressive theological reasoning to support the Church's position. There is none. Had I been asked about the marriage of priests after ordination or the marriage of Catholics after divorce, I would have replied in the negative and made the same assumptions. I would have responded in like manner, although in the affirmative, if I were asked whether the papacy as we have it is what Christ had in mind, including the prerogatives of infallibility and universal jurisdiction.

I once knew so much!

I once assumed so much! I, and the whole Catholic Church and the entire theological community with me.

We know now that there is no biblical evidence and no convincing theological reasoning to support any of these official positions.

Perhaps, on a bad day, I might have told the inquiring student that the question was without merit or academic validity and that approved authors should be followed in such instances. I would hope not but, perhaps, I might have at least felt that way. And, so, perhaps I can understand my colleague in Scripture to a degree. The problem, however, lies in responding in the present as we would have many decades ago. The official Church uses the same assumptions it used in the past to deal with these issues even though all these assumptions have been disproven not only by the best and the brightest scholars in our Church but also by overwhelming numbers of priests in pastoral ministry and by laity throughout the world.

I would like to share one more personal item before we look at the evidence before us on the marriage of Jesus. It seems to me that the official Church position on mandatory celibacy has no biblical, theological or pastoral support for it. The vast majority of theologians would concur with this. There are, however, three arguments beyond these which the Vatican continues to use to discredit and shame priests who marry after they have been ordained.

This is my third major address at a Corpus National Conference. In each of these, I have dealt, in turn, with all three Vatican charges.

1. In "Broken Promises," Washington, D.C., 1988, I reflected on whether married priests were men of broken promises and shattered vows.

2. In "Redeeming Humanity," New York City, 1991, I looked at the history and the motives which led to mandatory celibacy and questioned whether the intent and the consequence were truly a spiritually superior and pastorally more responsive priesthood.

3. In this Conference, here at Kent State, Ohio, 1995, with "Joseph's Son," I wish to address the question of whether Jesus never married and the aftereffect which follows this, namely, that a married person does not image and imitate Jesus as effectively as a celibate does.

If there continue to be married priests, their parents, spouses, children or friends who are shamed and embarrassed, it is totally due, I believe, to assumptions they internalized as oppression. These assumptions are that priests who marry after ordination break their promises, surrender a superior call to celibacy for an inferior vocation, and follow Christ less ardently.

The official Church has, as we have said, no biblical arguments, theological reasoning or pastoral benefits to support its present policy on mandatory celibacy. The policy has become almost absurd in its full articulation. It reads as follows: Celibacy is mandatory for all priests of the Latin Rite who were not Protestants first or who, if they are Catholics, have not yet divorced their wives, separated from them sexually, or buried them.

Having no biblical, theological or pastoral justification for the idiosyncratic law of mandatory celibacy, the official Church uses psychological shame as a weapon. The word "weapon" is not lightly chosen because the wounds inflicted are often painful, permanent, and lethal. For a sensitive priest to be told he is unfaithful to his promises, self-indulgent in choosing a sexual relationship over celibate spirituality and less a disciple of the unmarried Christ is to open the possibility of silencing, shaming and shackling not only his voice but his very heart and soul. This pain often wounds his spouse, children and friends.

THE EVIDENCE

The title of this talk is "Joseph's Son." I chose that title partly to distance Jesus from too much an emphasis on his being "Mary's Son." Traditionally, we have associated Mary with virginity, immaculate conception and assumption; we have celebrated her as "Mother of God" and "Queen of Heaven." "To the extent that Jesus is "Mary's Son," he is more readily seen as divine and other-worldly, angelic and ascetic. One moves easily from the virginity of Mary to the celibacy of Jesus, from son of Mary to Son of God.

There is no need for us now to challenge the development of Marian privileges. Mary's role in the scheme of things has been magnified far beyond Paul's description of Jesus as "born of a woman" unnamed and far beyond the Gospels which do not make her the most significant woman in the New Testament. None of this is an attempt to dishonor the identity of Mary or to make less of the Sonship of Christ with God.

But with Joseph, there is a different resonance to Jesus. We move, in Matthew's genealogy, from the sexual relationship of Abraham and Sarah to the seed of David and on to Joseph and Jesus. In Joseph's mind, Mary was guilty of adultery and he had decided to divorce her. One has the impression that Joseph desired a sexual relationship with Mary and that he was grieved that she had experienced sex with someone else.

With Joseph, Jesus is not as much the child of a virgin but the carpenter's son.

None of what I have said about Joseph is a later development. All of this is in the New Testament.

The earliest writings provide intriguing information on the family life of Jesus. Paul says nothing of Mary and seems to know nothing of her virginity or of a miraculous conception. Mark, the first Gospel, makes no reference to anything unusual about the biological origins of Jesus. He gives the impression that there were at least seven children born to Mary and Joseph and he names them (6:3). There were five sons: Jesus, James, Joset, Jude, Simon; there are, at least, two sisters. Paul tells us more, namely, that the brothers of Jesus are married and take their wives with them on missionary journeys (I Corinthians 9:5). Mark also adds that Jesus is a "carpenter."

Later Catholic theology will make these brothers of Jesus cousins, without evidence, in an effort to declare Mary a life-long virgin. One wonders what is gained by this. Most people find a completely sexless marriage bizarre when a sexual relationship is possible. It is instructive to realize that this sexless marriage is developed as doctrine in the same period when married priests are being warned by Church officials to keep their marriages sexless. We must not miss this constant transferal from doctrine to discipline, from teaching about the virginity of Mary and the celibacy of Christ to insistence on the same for clerics, monks, hermits, and nuns. In any case, the sexless marriage between Mary and Joseph will be utilized to protect our later Christology and to project on the Church a spiritual asceticism which is closer to the philosophy of Plato than it is to the teaching of Jesus.

There is no indication that Mary and Joseph had intended a celibate marriage. It seems to have been God's idea because Joseph is confused and Mary is astonished by the revelation that a sexual relationship will not occur in this marriage.

If it is God's idea that celibacy is an ideal way to live and that only a sexless marriage is fitting for the conception of Jesus, God's behavior through biblical history is unusual and unhelpful.

We learn in the first chapter of Genesis that reproductive sexuality is God's first idea and first commandment to the man and woman made in the divine image and likeness. God apparently did not fear that the divine image would be lost in a sexual relationship or enhanced in a celibate marriage. Why, then, one wonders, would the divinity of Jesus not be able to survive the sexual love of Mary and Joseph?

In the second chapter of Genesis, there is more. The first time God finds something "not good" in the Bible, it is the celibacy of Adam. I do not say this to denigrate celibacy. I celebrate optional celibacy. Adam's celibacy, however, is not optional and God reasons that this is "not good" for the man to be alone. The reproductive sexuality of Genesis 1, "Increase and multiply," is transformed into the psychological sexuality of Genesis 2.

For a woman, a man will leave his father and mother, even a Church discipline and prohibition, we might add. The woman is worth this. The husband will cleave to his wife and they will become one flesh and feel no shame. God wants no shame when a man loves a woman. How differently will Augustine write later about the sexual love of husband and wife! Why did we hear him and not Genesis?

Adam's sexual joy is lyrical. The woman is bone of my bone, flesh of my flesh, he says. I will leave everything and everyone for her.

In the remainder of the Hebrew Bible, there is not a single instance of freely chosen life-long celibacy. No patriarch or matriarch, no prophet or king chooses such celibacy as a way of pleasing God. God seems neither to want nor bless this celibacy. It is worth noting that this is the only Bible Jesus will have available to him. It is also helpful to realize that Jesus will quote approvingly from Genesis, not from the first chapter about reproductive sexuality but from the second chapter about psychological and sexual bonding. Jesus is not scandalized or embarrassed by marital love-making the way Origen, Jerome and Augustine will be.

If God and, later, Jesus, wanted us to see sexless marriages and life-long celibacy as an ideal, this is a strange way to prepare us for it.

A few Catholic writers try to make a great deal of the celibacy of Jeremiah. The celibacy of Jeremiah, however, is only temporary and is related to punishment. In Jeremiah 16:1-4, the prophet is told not to marry or have children "in this place." God asks this of Jeremiah so that the distortion of celibacy will convince God's People that something is wrong between them and God. This is sexual abstinence presented as a warning of an impending national disaster, not an invitation to a life of spiritual excellence and ideal ministerial service.

As Jesus comes of age, neither he nor Joseph have a single image of life-long celibacy as an ideal from the Hebrew Bible to guide them. It is true that, in some instances, Jesus will depart from the Hebrew Bible. He does so in rejecting violence. But the Hebrew Bible speaks at least, on occasion, about a time of universal peace. The New Testament gives us clear teaching about the exceptions Jesus makes to the Hebrew Bible.

But the New Testament is lacking in any model or any clear teaching of life-long celibacy as an ideal for the Christian community.

If Joseph were to prepare Jesus for a life of celibacy, he had no help from the Scriptures. As we shall see, it was the father's duty to teach his sons the Torah.

It is now time to look at the celibacy of Jesus.

THE CELIBACY OF JESUS

The Gospels never state that Jesus claims he is a celibate or the son of a virgin. Nowhere else in the New Testament does anyone say Jesus is a celibate. If life-long celibacy is so important to preserve the uniqueness of Jesus, as official Church teaching now insists, why did not at least one New Testament writer or one Gospel make a point of this somewhere?

Let us try to recreate the climate or environment in which Jesus came of age by utilizing the Hebrew Bible and the second century Mishnah which collects oral traditions going back to the time of Jesus.

We read in the Mishnah that there are five tasks a father must accomplish for his son:

He must circumcise him, redeem him, instruct him in the Torah, teach him a trade and find a wife for him.

The New Testament shows that Jesus is made the recipient of four of these five benefits:

1. Circumcision is mentioned in Luke 2:21. Circumcision was associated with fitness for marriage. Philo writes that it facilitated intercourse. Martin Buber calls circumcision the sacrament of the consecration of the body and the sacrament of sexual intercourse.

2. Redemption or Consecration of the First-Born. This is described in Luke 2:22-25. It includes animal sacrifice in remembrance of God's setting Israel free from bondage (Exodus 13:11-15; purification regulations in Leviticus 12:2-8).

3. Knowledge of the Torah is clear from Luke 2:48-49. Joseph is still alive, of course, during this Temple scene. The Torah, as we know, commands marriage and blesses sexual intercourse.

4. Instruction in a Trade. Matthew calls Jesus "the carpenter's son"(13:55). Mark calls Jesus himself "the carpenter"(6:13).

There is one item missing.

In Judaism at the time a wife was selected for a son soon after puberty. Arrangements were made between both fathers with little consultation with the future spouses. The father of the young man was the principal actor because the wife joined his family. The father of the young man paid the bridal price because the son would have no money of his own.

Luke tells us Jesus obeyed his parents (2:51). How likely is it that Jesus did not marry at that time?

Had Jesus refused to marry and had he declared himself a life-long celibate, a behavior so unusual, so much against all Jewish custom and law, would surely have been recorded somewhere in the New Testament.

The general rule in human affairs is that out of the ordinary behavior is etched in the memory, gets talked about, and transmitted. Ordinary behavior is taken for granted and receives no comment.

Life-long celibacy would have been so extraordinary, confusing, and troublesome for his contemporaries that had Jesus so lived it is unlikely this would not have been noted somewhere.

COMING OF AGE

Jesus grew into maturity in a culture which presupposed marriage and supported it. A pious young Jewish man would see marriage as a way of pleasing God.

The Mishnah warns: When a bachelor attains the age of twenty and is unmarried, the Holy One says: "Let him perish."

Indeed, the Mishnah counsels that "an unmarried man may not be a teacher of children"(Kiddushin 4,13).

The Mishnah forbids living without a spouse unless one has already married and begotten children.

Had Jesus been a widower it would have been acceptable for him to remain unmarried during his ministry. Not otherwise.

We might give other examples but it seems clear that Jesus is part of a culture which identified holiness with marital sexuality and not with its renunciation. Indeed, marriage was intimately bound up with life's very purpose. It continued the human race and made it as much a community as it is likely to be. It regulated sexual life and safeguarded the vulnerable from sexual predators.

It was only after learning the Torah, taking up a trade and entering marriage that a man was deemed mature and fit, at about the age of thirty, to become a teacher of others.

As Jesus learns the Torah, he finds there that all Israel's great models for behavior and holiness are married people. The greatest patriarch, Abraham, is married, as are all the other patriarchs. The greatest leader of Israel, Moses, its law giver, in a sense, the founder of its religion is married. David, the greatest king, and Solomon, his son, are married, as are all other kings. The greatest prophet, Isaiah, is married and, almost certainly, all the other prophets.

Abraham did not require sexual renunciation before he could become Israel's great model of faith. Moses could behold the face of God and reach sublime heights of mystical union with God as a married man. The psalms did not come from a celibate nor did the soaring love of God expressed by the prophets.

Later Catholic theology will suggest that all these marriages are concessions to human weakness and that God always intended celibacy as the ideal way to live. Where is the evidence for this or the sense of it?

When we reach the New Testament, Peter, the greatest of the Twelve, is married. We know this only from the most incidental information: the curing of his mother-in-law and the observations of Paul (I Corinthians 9:5) about Peter traveling with his wife. Had these incidental items not found their way into the canon, there would have been volumes written by Catholic scholars celebrating the celibacy of Peter and, no doubt, attributing Peter's special place among the Twelve to it. The information we have on Peter is incidental because, as we have said before, it is assumed that people are married.

In this light, it is difficult to imagine that all the other apostles were not married. Why would they not be?

The sayings of Jesus about leaving family and even hating it are clearly hyperbole because the New Testament and subsequent Christian history do not endorse a literal interpretation of this teaching. Jesus reminds his hearers of the need to honor father and mother and he reprimands the Pharisees for using legalism to avoid caring for them when they are old. The author of Ephesians asks husbands and wives to love each other and Paul reminds the Corinthians not to neglect sexual love in marriage for too long a time. Sexual love is presented in Ephesians as the best of symbols for manifesting Christ's love for the Church. Where, in all this, is there a summons to sexual renunciation as an ideal?

If Jesus called for celibacy, why would the letters to Timothy and Titus give marriage as a necessary precondition for Church office or in I Timothy 4:1-3 equate the prohibition of marriage with a demonic influence in the Church.

If all of Jesus' circle were unmarried they would be seen as a danger and a scandal. It is difficult to believe that the people of Jesus' time, or ours, would find fitting a large group of unmarried men and young virginal women traveling about Israel day and night and living in close quarters with one another. Paul tells us in I Corinthians 9:5 that Christian missionaries, some twenty years after Jesus, went on the road as couples. This may well be because they did this when Jesus was with them.

In preparing for this talk, I wrote to a prominent Biblical scholar, an expert on Paul, and asked why it is that Jesus, by living supposedly as a life-long celibate, is not charged with violating God's command. Jesus is charged by his adversaries with serious failings in many other aspects of his life. Why not this? My colleague, who asked not to be quoted by name, conjectured that Jesus was married or had once been married.

The Essenes who are not mentioned in the New Testament are not charged with violations of God's intent because their celibacy is temporary and, in a number of cases, they are widowed. In any case, Essene spirituality is vastly different from that of Jesus. Jesus does not divide the world sharply into hostile and friendly zones. Nor does he invite his disciples to leave the world and prepare for battle. He is not preoccupied with apocalyptic visions of the end time as a primary focus of his ministry.

I find it disappointing that two very prominent Catholic Biblical scholars dismiss the marriage of Jesus as even a possibility on the basis of extraordinarily flimsy evidence. One of these equates the question with novel writing rather than serious study. Yet, it seems to me we not only claim that Jesus is celibate but that this is certain and we do so without a shred of evidence. Does not the evidence for marriage amount to a possibility if not a probability?

The second writer claims Jesus did not marry because he was too poor. I find this curious. If Joseph was not too poor to marry might not we assume that Jesus, some fifteen years later, would not be? It is, of course, possible Jesus was too poor to marry but it is highly unlikely. It is strange to exclude a possibility of marriage on this basis alone. Even desperately poor people have managed to marry, not only in the past but also now.

This tendency to reach definitive conclusions against substantial evidence to the contrary is not unknown in Catholic and papal circles.

When Pope Paul VI, two years after Vatican II, insisted on mandatory celibacy for priests in the Latin Rite, he wrote in his 1967 encyclical, *Sacerdotalis Celibatus*:

> *Christ remained throughout his whole life in a state of celibacy which signified his total dedication to the service of God and people…(Priests) will be more perfect the more free the sacred minister is from the bonds of flesh and blood (par. 21).*

The number of problems in these two sentences is astonishing. How does the pope know Christ was always celibate? To declare, furthermore, that celibacy is a sign of total dedication implies that marriage is less. Was Peter not totally dedicated to Christ? Would celibacy have been necessary for him to serve God fully? Were Moses and Isaiah less than they might have been because they married? Was Adam in a better state without Eve? After the Fall, God does not ask Adam and Eve to remain celibate. It would seem that marriage does not diminish dedication to God. If it does, why do we call it a symbol of Christ's total love for the Church?

To teach, furthermore, that priests are more perfect the more they are removed from flesh and blood is a form of Gnosticism. It seems to go against everything we intend by the doctrine of the Incarnation. It invites the development of a dreadful spirituality, one in which every effort will be made to deny our humanity.

Should we not conclude that God should have become an angelic spirit to lead us rather than a human being? Would the priesthood fare better if it were made up of angels rather than people?

How could the pope send out such a letter to the Church at large?

These observations of Pope Paul are instructive in other ways. The movement from a celibate Christ to a mandatory law of celibacy for priests should not be missed by the reader.

Christians are prepared to accept a Jesus who is like us in all ways except sexual experience. For many, it is not unfitting for Jesus to be weary, discouraged, hungry, angry, thirsty, sorrowful. The line is drawn, however, when sexual realities are discussed. The letter to the Hebrews, however, observes that Christ can "sympathize with our weaknesses" because "in every respect" he has been tested or tempted as we have been (4:15-16). On what basis do we make exceptions to the clear biblical evidence? Why do we do this? Consider the clarity of Hebrews 2:14-17:

> *Since (we) share flesh and blood, he himself shared the same things... For it is clear he did not come to help angels but descendants of Abraham. Therefore he had to become like his brothers and sisters in every respect so that he might be a merciful and faithful high priest...*

THE SECOND CENTURY

The life-long celibacy of Mary and Christ became the subject of speculation and then of certitude beginning in the second century. The second century brings three massive changes into the growing Christian community:

▶ The destruction of Jerusalem leads to fewer Jewish Church leaders; such leaders were more disposed to marriage as a source of holiness and as a part of God's original design for creation.

▶ Gentile leaders, molded by Greco-Roman culture, tend to equate spirituality with a denial of all physical pleasure.

▶ The Roman persecutions dispose Christians to equate martyrdom or its equivalent in sexual renunciation with an ideal way of serving God; sacrifice is emphasized over service.

In an earlier conference, I dealt with the almost pathological denial of sexuality and the emergence of misogyny in the second to the fifth century Christian community. This essay, Redeeming Humanity which can be found on page 159.

Origen writes, early in this period: "Whoever, after the conjugal act...approaches boldly to receive the Eucharistic bread dishonors and profanes what is holy." *(Ezechiel Selections 7)* It is difficult to imagine Jesus saying this to the disciples at the Last Supper.

Origen reasons that the dry virginal womb of Mary, not moistened by semen *(Genesis Homilies, 17)*, is predicted by Isaiah 53:2 where we read that the suffering servant will grow up "like a root out of arid ground." This is a bit much.

The New Testament tension between egocentric self-will and the call to love others is transformed during the second to the fifth centuries into a battle between flesh and spirit. Church leaders equate flesh, especially physical pleasure, with sin, and present spirit as the sole source of holiness.

Augustine writes in *The Good of Marriage* (10) that if all human beings were celibate the human race would end sooner and the welcome Reign of God would come more quickly.

Gregory of Nyssa laments that his marriage has robbed him of the possibility of life-long celibacy.

The metaphor of Christ as Bridegroom and the Church as Bride, a beautiful image, is now interpreted literally. Christ is truly married to the Church so that marriage to a woman is seen as adultery if it is a priest "another Christ," who makes the choice.

If we applied metaphors literally in other instances we would have to conclude that Jesus was a door or a lamp.

These foolish notions by otherwise intelligent people cause me to wonder about the sexual fears and pathologies in many who promote obligatory celibacy. This is, of course, not true of all. Nor does it diminish in the slightest the beauty and value of freely chosen celibacy.

Sometimes sexual repression surfaces in lurid ways. Jerome writes the following to a group of young women:

Ever let the Bridegroom sport with you...he will come ...and will touch your body and you will arise trembling and cry, "I am lovesick,"...Jesus is jealous. He does not wish your face to be seen by others (Letters 22, 25).

Augustine finds Mary's virginity predicted many centuries before by Ezechiel. Augustine believes Mary was a virgin before, during and after the birth of Jesus. He is preoccupied with the condition of the vagina in the interpretation of virginity. Augustine quotes Ezechiel 44:2 and applies it to Mary's body in a way that says more of Augustine than it does of Ezechiel or Mary:

This gate shall remain shut. It shall not be opened and no man shall pass through it; because the Lord God of Israel has entered it.

In *The City Of God*, Augustine speculates what sex would have been like if there had not been a Fall. He reasons that women would have remained virgins with their hymens intact. He, therefore, conjectures that men would have had orgasms outside the vagina and that gravity would have carried semen to its proper place where conception could occur. Thus all sex would have been virginal and intercourse need not ever have occurred.

What makes otherwise brilliant men engage in such folly?

This is the time frame when theologians and Church leaders insist on the perpetual virginity of Mary and the life- long celibacy of Jesus. It is not a period when thinking about sexuality is healthy, holy or even biblical.

APPLICATIONS

In this concluding section, I would like to consider a number of questions.

1. Was Jesus married?

On the basis of the evidence offered, I would say there is a high probability that he was. There is no certainty here of course. There may never be. The evidence for the life-long celibacy of Jesus is non-existent. Yet Church leaders are certain he was.

I wonder if we all might be a bit more humble and tentative about this issue.

2. Is this a pointless question?

The point about whether Jesus was married would be less significant had the institutional Church not made an industry of his assumed celibacy. It did this in two areas of Church life. It used the celibacy of Jesus, which was free and a gift if it did exist, to fortify a law of mandatory celibacy and to shame and punish those who deviated from it. Surely Jesus, even a celibate Jesus, would not have wanted this consequence from his celibacy. I believe we have covered this issue sufficiently in this talk.

I would like to spend a moment considering another unwarranted use of these matters by the institutional Church.

The perpetual virginity of Mary and Jesus have been employed to implant deep in the Catholic psyche a fear of sex and shame about it. This fear and shame exist in other Churches, religions, and societies, of course, but they take on a special vehemence in Catholicism. Here, sexless marriages may be promoted and a sexless priesthood is presented as an ideal. Here, masturbation is seen as a grave sin and artificial birth control as a perversion of nature.

Many married priests struggle to regain their dignity and self-esteem when they move from the supposed ideal state of celibacy to the shameful experience of sex. Many Catholic laity are encouraged to believe that a priest married after ordination even with dispensation from celibacy and permission from the pope to marry is to be held in contempt and dishonor. If, however, he divorces his wife or she dies and he returns with a celibate commitment he is held in honor and esteem.

There is healthy teaching elsewhere in the Christian Community.

In I Timothy 4:13 we read that the prohibition of marriage is a demonic doctrine. Luther writes: "Next to God's Word there is no more precious treasure than holy matrimony." John Calvin, in his commentary on First Corinthians, writes:

> It was later than the apostles that men lit upon the remarkable piece of wisdom that the priests of the Lord are defiled if they have intercourse with their lawful wives. At last it went so far that Pope Siricius had no hesitation about calling marriage "an uncleanness of the flesh in which no one can please God." What, then, will happen to the unfortunate apostles, who persisted in this impurity until their death?

Erasmus, by many accounts the most brilliant thinker in sixteenth century Europe, a Catholic and the son of a priest, argues:

> Should not marriage be honored above all sacraments because it was the first to be instituted ... The other sacraments were established on earth, this one in Paradise ... the others were ordained for fallen nature but this one for nature unspoiled ... I would like to see permission given to priests and monks to marry .. Why refrain from that which God institutes, nature sanctions, reason persuades, divine and human laws approve, the consent of all nations endorses ... (Erasmus of Christendom, R. H. Bainton, NY, 1969, 49-50).

In this same period, the Council of Trent teaches what it foresees as permanent Catholic doctrine. It denounces and anathematizes those who call into question the superiority of celibacy to marriage (D S 1810).

3. Why is the wife of Jesus, if he indeed married, or his children not mentioned in the New Testament?

The New Testament does not name spouses as a general rule unless they have done something prominent in their own right. We do not know the name of Peter's wife although she is still traveling with him some twenty years after the crucifixion during the last decade or so of Peter's life.

We do not know the names of the wives of the other apostles. The New Testament simply assumes their marriages.

The Hebrew Bible, of course, assumes the same. Further information is only given if significant. We only know the names of Isaiah's children, for example, because their names were titles of their father's sermons. (Isaiah 7 and 8)

4. If he married, who was the wife of Jesus?

We do not know.Magdalene has been named at times throughout Christian history. The second-century non-canonical Gospel of Philip states that Magdalene was the wife of Jesus and Jesus was conceived in the normal manner.

I am merely noting this, not claiming it.

Some intriguing things are said about Magdalene in the canonical Gospels. She is the only person named in all four Gospels as having been at the cross until the end. Generally, only relatives were allowed near a crucified criminal. She is the only person named in all four Gospels as having first come to the tomb on Easter morning. She does so to fulfill the task of the wife or relatives of the deceased person, namely, the anointing of the body.

None of this is conclusive; all of it is instructive.

In Catholic theology, we make much of the fact that Peter's name is always first when the apostles are listed. Magdalene's name is also first in the Synoptic Gospels whenever the women disciples are named. (Mk. 15:40-41; Mk. 16:1; Mk. 16:9; Mt. 27:56; Mt. 28:1; Lk. 8:2; Lk. 24:10)

I believe the most beautiful Easter story is the intimate encounter between Jesus and Magdalene in John 20. She recognizes him by the way he says her name.

Jesus asks Mary not to continue to cling to him. The Latin translation of Jerome diminished the force of the Greek text. Jerome's text was the only one approved by the Church, other than the Greek text, for one thousand years. Jerome has Jesus tell Magdalene: "Noli me tangere."("Do not touch me.") This left the impression that the Risen Christ did not want anyone to touch his spiritual body.

We know that this is incorrect because Jesus, in the same Gospel, invites doubting Thomas to touch and handle him.

The Greek text is instructive. The Greek verb is "APTO." This is a much more intensely physical word than the Latin "tangere." The verb means "to fasten," "to cling closely." It was used in Greek to describe fastening a shield. It is used by Paul, in a sexual sense, when he writes about a man not touching a woman (I *Corinthians* 7:1). The verb need not have that meaning. As in English, "touch" or "hold on to" can denote non-sexual contact. Mark uses the verb in this sense when a woman touches the cloak of Jesus. (Mark 5:27).

The form of the verb in Greek has an ongoing or continuous dimension to it. It is not unfaithful to the text to have Jesus say: "Do not continue holding on to me any longer.. But go to my brothers and say to them…

The Greek is stronger than Jerome's "Do not touch me."

Again we must not make too much of this or reach conclusions beyond the evidence. The Greek verb, however, has the potential of expressing an intense passionate, emotional holding, not necessarily sexual, but clearly denoting a deep intimacy between Jesus and Mary. This closeness may be that of a family member or beloved disciple. In any case, it is more than "Do not touch me." I cannot suggest one definitive interpretation but I think the clinging of Mary to Jesus adds enormously to the beauty of the text. Women felt comfortable anointing his feet or sitting near him as Mary does in the Martha-Mary story.

A Magdalene who clings to the Risen Christ represents the resurrection of all women from the inferior status patriarchy had afforded them. It is sad, indeed, that our iconography never portrays Mary, the wife of Joseph, and Joseph, her husband, in an embrace. Whether they had a sexual relationship or not, did they never embrace? If they did not, was their relationship truly human or marital? If they did, why do we never show this? Indeed, in Catholic Churches we keep Mary and Joseph apart, at separate altars. Did Jesus never see his parents embrace or show tenderness to each other?

The text we consider tells us that Magdalene clung to Jesus, possibly the way a shipwrecked survivor clings to shore. Such a beautiful image! The woman who saw all the agony of his dying and who died a thousands times as he died now clings to her Savior, now finds him alive after all her hopes seemed to have been buried. What a pity to reduce this text to the weak and anemic, "Do not touch me." How sad it is that we have no icons or paintings which show Magdalene and Jesus embracing on Easter morning! Magdalene clinging to Jesus represents all of us, overjoyed by the Easter life of Jesus, holding on to someone we love and on whom all our hope rests.

5. Did Jesus have Children?

We do not know.

We do know that if he did, they were not prominent in the New Testament Church. The New Testament names spouses and children when they are important members of the community in their own right.

Some Catholics and Protestant thinkers have stated that Jesus could not have children without their being half-divine, half-human.

One would think, however, that if Jesus is fully human, then his humanity would generate human children. The humanity of Jesus maintains its own integrity and remains intact in its own right.

6. Why do people react so strongly against the idea or possibility of Jesus being married?

Such a reaction tells us a great deal about people and little if anything about the issue.

I find most disturbing not the fact that Jesus was always celibate but that some see no alternative to this. If Jesus can only be all-holy if he is celibate and if he is defiled if he married, then we have made a devastating evaluation of marriage. It is also disturbing to find something intrinsically healthy and spiritual in a sexless marriage between Mary and Joseph. A marriage may or may not have a sexless component to it. This is very different from affirming that a sexless marriage is superior.

7. Is this question important for the emergence of a married priesthood for Latin Rite, life-long Catholics in the Church?

I think it is.

People do feel a sense of shame about sex in different cultures around the world. This may have something to do with our confusion about menstruation or unintended sexual feelings. Whatever the source, a measure of diffidence is not unhealthy in such a personal, intimate and private experience. In sexual experience people are vulnerable; it is not easy to have one's vulnerability indiscriminately exposed.

In the West, especially, this shame is tied up with guilt, sinfulness, and inferiority. Certainly, none of this is from Jesus.

If many people identify sex with sin and with the darker side of their psyche, and if they identify Jesus with holiness and with all that is best about them, then a married Jesus may redeem sexuality tellingly from its supposed demonic and negative characteristics and make it worthy of God in the eyes of all. Conversely, a Jesus who is presented as shunning all sexual commitments and doing so because they are unworthy may reinforce fears that sex is not good.

The reason why some Catholics are deeply upset by priests who marry may have something to do with their ambivalence about a priesthood identified with holiness wedded to a sexuality identified with sin. A married priest may, in the final analysis, redeem sex from some of the negativity associated with it in the Catholic community.

The married priest helps shatter the Berlin Wall of ministerial service Church leaders have built and patrol, keeping women and married Christians on one side and male, celibate priests on the other. It is time to make the Church an undivided community led by pastors whose gender or marital status alone do not determine inclusion or exclusion.

Church leaders at times are compelled to speak of women in courteous terms, granting them respect but no equality. This is no longer sufficient. Church documents refer to marriage in language whose rhetoric is impressive, giving marriage a certain respectability but no authority in the Church. This is no longer adequate. And so we have raised the question. Let us make of it what we will.

I am asking the reader to consider the cumulative force of all the evidence assembled and not to focus the entire issue on only one or another item. John Henry Newman wrote of a convergence of probabilities in some areas of life. This may be one of them.

Before we reject or accept the possibility or probability of a married Jesus, we must also ask what the evidence offered for the life-long celibacy of Jesus is and whether it is as convincing as we once thought.

CONCLUSION

Is it not a pity that we did not grow up in a Church in which we were told that sexuality is holy and that all children are immaculately conceived?

Is it not a pity that we were not given a Christ who as Son of God would not have been made less worthy for having loved a wife, whether or not he chose to marry? Is it not a pity that we live in a Church where we are taught to reject married priests and their ministry and to punish the women who have become the mothers of their sons and daughters?

Is it not more the pity that we are told Christ is pleased with this policy?

Is it not a pity that a colleague of mine at Notre Dame could not bear to think of a married Jesus as God's Son, and nonetheless, still worthy of all his love?

Is it not a pity that the widows of married priests must fear even to the end that their husbands will not be blessed and buried with honor by this Church?

Is it not a pity that we do not see more shame in this than in the sexual love of married priests and their wives?

Is it not a pity that the wives of married priests must proceed cautiously in this Church, never celebrated for who they are no matter how many children the bear, no matter how much they love, no matter how good they are?

None of this is from Christ. None of it. For this reason the pity is all the more painful.

Is it not a pity that married priests, only because they have married, hesitate to affirm their priesthood again? Is it not a pity that their terrified, celibate priest brothers find it difficult to invite them to the altar once more?

Is it not a pity that the evil of mandatory celibacy is not preached by priests and proclaimed by bishops?

I believe that mandatory celibacy may have done as much or more evil than any other Church policy, especially when one considers all its consequences in terms of the exclusion of women and the negative reading it gives the laity on sexuality.

Is it not a pity that we live in a Church unwilling to consider that the Son of God may have made sexuality a sacrament and redeemed the human body by loving a woman?

Could it be that Jesus himself, our savior, felt passion for a woman and reached out in love to her? Is this unworthy of God? Why?

None of this may have happened. But why is it obscene and blasphemous and traitorous and irreverent and self—serving to think so?

Is it not a pity that we live in a Church which once believed that God was pleased with our Inquisitions and Crusades but offended by the thought he might have loved a woman?

When Jesus cried out: "Have you not heard that God made one flesh out of two, bone of bone, blood of blood?" might he not have had in mind a face, a memory, a name? Why is this unworthy of God? Tell me.

Is it not more likely that a married Jesus would more easily equate the Reign of God with weddings, with the joy of the bridegroom, with the embrace of a lost son, with an expansive role for women, a role so magnanimous that two thousand years later the Church still does not equal it?

None of this is necessary but all of this is likely. Is it not? Is it not a pity that we do not allow Mary's child to become Joseph's son?

Is it not a pity that we have made so much of Peter, good Peter, but so little of Magdalene?

Magdalene's faith may be more than that of all the other apostles. She witnessed the death of Jesus in all the horror, agony, and finality of it. She knew the death better than the others. Only she of all the apostles came to the tomb in the first dawn of Easter morning. And so the glory of the Resurrection is hers in a special way.

Magdalene fulfilled the criteria for being an apostle: she was with Jesus in the public ministry and she saw the Risen Christ.

What a pity it would be if married priests or celibate priests felt a need to walk away from the table because the marriage of Jesus was discussed.

Jesus as bridegroom or celibate, whatever is necessary, invites all to the table. There are no privileged places at the table, certainly not by virtue of gender or marital status. At a family table, gender or marital status never matter, only presence. The sole dishonor at a family table is an empty chair. The worst sin is arbitrary dismissal from the table.

We have been called to a banquet, my friends, a wedding feast. The joy is not in the wine which does not give out or in the bread forever multiplied or in the dance of life. The joy is in the fact that there is a place now for all of us.

The joy is in the realization we have that a time of pity in the Church has run its course and a season of compassion has arrived. The joy is in knowing that everyone whose hands are empty and whose hearts are needy has been called home.

The Exodus is over, the pity has passed, the slavery has been annulled, the shame has been banished, the Promised Land is in sight, the Vatican Council has risen from its crucifixion by some misguided Church leaders, the Spirit is everywhere and every man and woman, married or celibate, has been called to become a lover.

17

Redeeming Humanity

Late in the second century, a seventeen-year old son wrote to his father, Leonides, awaiting martyrdom for the sake of Christ. The letter urged him to go to his death bravely, with no anxiety for his family of seven children.

The young man himself yearned to die as a martyr. His mother barely kept him steady and hid his clothes to prevent him from begging the Romans to kill him. The young man was brilliant but volatile and erratic.

He defined himself as the "son of a martyr," a title he treasured. He grew despondent, however, as the opportunity for martyrdom receded and as his sexual temptations intensified.

Three years after his father's execution, the young man, now twenty, found a physician and asked to be castrated. In the blood of that mutilation, the young man believed his humanity was redeemed.

We are speaking of Origen, sometimes cited, with good reason, as one of the most brilliant thinkers who ever lived. But Origen is a troubled man living in a troubled century.

ORIGEN

Why this story? This essay will seek to document one of the main reasons why married priests and their wives made the decisions they did. It was to distance ourselves, I suggest, from the Church and spirituality represented by some of the events and the cast of characters we shall review. More than this, however, I hope to present an account which has meaning for all people in the Church. The married priesthood is worthy of attention only if the whole Church benefits from the issues it raises.

To evaluate the Origen story, we might raise a few questions. Why, for example, was the celibacy of Jesus so different from that of Origen? Why can we not imagine Jesus acting as Origen did or expecting his disciples to do such violence?

The difference lies in the fact that Jesus saw his celibacy as an item of minor significance and Origen considered celibacy the defining event of his life. Jesus was not primarily a celibate; he was a prophet whose celibacy made sense only in the context of prophecy and of his own personal life. Jesus makes no reference to his celibacy, and expects it of none of his disciples. A prophet or an apostle for that matter might just as well have been married, in the thinking of Jesus, as Isaiah was or as Peter is. The New Testament Church makes so little of the celibacy of Jesus that when Paul speaks of the excellence of celibacy, he makes no reference to the celibacy of Jesus. Jesus is a prophet, not *the* celibate. When Paul forcefully proclaims his celibacy to the Corinthians, he refrains from asking the Corinthian Church as a whole to follow his example. It is almost a century after Jesus before any of his disciples base their celibacy on his example.

By the time we get to Origen, celibacy becomes more important than prophecy or, worse, celibacy is the prophetic witness.

There is more to this issue. The difference between Jesus and Origen lies in their attitude toward the Spirit. Jesus believed the Spirit came to everyone and might lead a disciple in any marital direction. The quality of the heart was the substantive work of the Spirit, not conjugal or celibate choices. For Origen, the Spirit prefers celibates. A hierarchical order gains ground in the Christian community, based on authority and the renunciation of sexual experience. In the course of subsequent Church history, the alliance between authority and celibacy will continue.

The castration of Origen derives from an unhealthy admixture of arrogance and despair. The arrogance is the assumption that he could control the Holy Spirit by destroying his body and that he could become thereby a part of an elite celibate corps of distinguished Christians. The despair is in the supposition that the Holy Spirit does not love us unless we renounce ourselves and mutilate ourselves physically or emotionally. Origen's castration generates a sad and savage spirituality and, in the next generation, a Church of force and power.

Origen's celibacy is based on two themes the New Testament Church would have found bizarre. In the first instance, he uses his celibacy as a power base to support prophetic or apostolic leadership in the Church. Until Origen, pastoral care of the Church was given by married heads of households who function as the priests and bishops of the first two centuries. From Origen forward, the Church will be governed by celibates, by and large, by men without family life, living a lifestyle different from that of the Christian community at large, a lifestyle deemed superior and more spiritual. Origen's castration eventually cuts off married pastors from the life of the community.

A second theme in Origen changes the tradition. Origen teaches the supremacy of life-long virginity. Until Origen celibacy was a choice people might make after the death of a spouse rather than for their whole life. In this context, celibacy and marriage complemented each other and both might serve the pastoral office or the spiritual life equally well.

Why did Origen's thinking have such an impact? It was due, I believe, to an unusual convergence of culture and politics in the next two centuries. The culture of Greek asceticism became the fashionable way to redeem or develop one's humanity. Origen was attuned to the character of his time. This asceticism preferred martyrdom to life, the desert to the community, virginity to family, men to women. Within a century of Origen's death, Ambrose declares that all that is best in the teaching of Jesus is in Plato. Celibacy, he continues, is the one experience which distinguishes us from the beasts of the field. The writers of the New Testament would have been startled at the eccentric character of such assertions.

Politics also plays a role. Within a century, Christianity and the Roman Empire join forces. The church now uses law and power to enforce its ideals and to proclaim the Gospel.

It is time for another story.

AUGUSTINE

The woman had been with him since he was eighteen. Even then, she knew he was brilliant. Everyone knew this. A year after they began to live together, she had a son. Now after thirteen years, he told her she must go away, at a time when he and their son especially needed her. He chose never to write or even, for all we know, to speak her name after her departure, as though the refusal to name her would make it seem she never existed or made a difference.

He loved her, in his own way, more perhaps than he ever loved anyone else. The wound of her leaving never fully healed. It bled in different ways throughout his life, as guilt and loss, as anger and longing, as envy and insecurity. She was always there somehow, competing with God for his attention although neither she nor God saw themselves as competitors. The last words she spoke to him were a vow, that she would never love or live with any other man for the rest of her life. Five years after she left, the boy, whom the father kept, died at the age of seventeen.

The man, of course, is Augustine; the boy is Adeodatus; the woman is anonymous. We are in the fourth century.

Augustine dismissed his companion, driven not by a law of celibacy but by a psychological need to excel and become perfect. If you were Augustine, you would understand. His age found the body loathsome. He had been a Manichean for nine years and learned that the body was "blood and bile and flatulence and excrement ... a mold of defilement."Ambrose, his mentor, and he himself saw sex as a body function and could not link it with love or grace or relationship. Augustine, with his insatiable sexual appetites, saw the woman as a co-conspirator in lust. He cut off his sexual life with her as sharply as Origen had once done his own.

Augustine won a mighty victory over himself but there were victims. The institutional Church and clerical celibacy gain a mighty champion but a nameless woman and, perhaps, Adeodatus and even Augustine himself and indeed, the future Church may all have been wounded by the ordeal and the achievement. It is a question worth raising, is it not?

Augustine speaks of Adeodatus from time to time as the years accumulate. Some months before Adeodatus dies, he expresses his pride in the boy's intelligence; in the last book he writes, he speaks of his son as someone a father is happy to have surpassed him "in all things." But there is always the ambivalence. He conceived Adeodatus in wickedness. Even had he been married, that would not have helped. Augustine believed sex was always wrong. "I had no part in that boy," he writes, "except the sin." Fortunately, Adeodatus had died before Augustine wrote that sentence.

We must not become sentimental or naive. Augustine, as a married man, might have developed less effectively. Celibacy, after all, for many, is a creative way to live. Saints such as Francis of Assisi, mystics such as Teresa of Avila are remarkably impressive people.

The sadness of Augustine lies in the fact that the Church had created a climate of necessity about celibacy and Augustine became a driven man. The problem is not celibacy but the fact that Augustine saw no meaningful alternative to it.

By the end of the fourth century, as a result of Origen and Augustine, respect of marriage has vanished; the value Jesus gave women in his preaching is gone.

"How sordid, filthy and horrible a woman's embraces," Augustine writes of wives. Hear the anger in the words. Yet Augustine is honest enough to express the ambivalence. During the day, he tells us, he is sure sex is evil but at night, as he lays awake and reviews what he has preached, he wonders if he is right and if things are so one-sided.

A final vignette of Augustine. Near the end of his life, he conducts a bitter debate with Julian, a bishop who espouses Pleagianism. Pelagianism asserts that people are basically good even without baptism. Augustine vigorously disagrees. Seldom in Church history do we behold a great and brilliant man so much at the mercy of his blind spots. Julian was the son of a bishop and married the daughter of a bishop. Allow me to summarize the debate.

Julian

If you are right, Augustine, that original sin is in our very nature, it seems the devil is as much a maker of human beings as God. Do I hear in this the Manicheanism you once accepted? When you declare without equivocation that all newborn children are evil until baptized, I shudder. When you add that you have found the source of evil and it is in our genitals, I am disgusted, affronted by this insult to God, our Creator.

Augustine

All human beings, infants included, are lost without baptism. God does not redeem humanity, only the elect. The proof that evil is in our genitals is our shame and, especially, those sexual feelings which stir us against our better judgment, reflecting the disobedience of a higher law which Adam initiated.

Julian

Sexual feeling is not evil. It is a sense in our body, like seeing or hearing, put there by God to make us aware of who we are.

Augustine

If people listen to you, Julian, they will "jump into bed whenever they like...tickled by desire" unable to wait until dark. Is this what you want for God's people? I hear not the voice of truth but the sort of sexual life you and your wife lead. Keep your sexual experience out of this debate.

Julian

We're not arguing about sex but about God. Your God punishes infants in eternal fire. Where is your compassion, your common sense? A God who tortures infants commits a crime disgusting to barbarians, let alone Christians.

Augustine

If unbaptized infants are saved, God is not sovereign. If human nature is good, why did Christ redeem us? If salvation is easy, what is the worth of our sacrifices, the women we send away, the children we do not generate, the sexual pleasure we reject?

Augustine's view prevails with Rome and the papacy. The anger and irrationality of Augustine in this debate are disturbing. How could so great a man, capable of generosity and warmth, become so savage? Is it because Julian was the son of a bishop and was himself about the same age as Adeodatus would have been had he lived? Was the real adversary not Julian but Augustine himself? Was the anger directed not at false teaching but at forced celibacy?

By the end of the fourth century, celibacy is the prestigious and spiritually superior life choice for a priest.

Who brought this to pass? Primarily, Origen and Augustine, even though there were many others. Origen and Augustine show how successful men of social position and elite education can live in cities and become spiritually exalted through celibacy, and substantial personal sacrifices. Both men are also talented publicists of their own lives and theories.

Why did this occur?

A cast of characters, including hermits and desert ascetics, bishops such as John Chrysostom and scholars such as Jerome, bring the Greek fear of the body, sex and women into the Church and give it respectability and status. Christianity's powerful influence in the Roman Empire allows it the resources and legal potential to institutionalize celibacy as the preferred alternative for a cleric. Since Christianity controls Western and Eastern Europe, celibacy brings enormous career and economic advantages. Even marriage is considered holy only insofar as it approximates the celibate ideal. The best marriages for all Christians are those which are sexless; in the marriages of clerics, this sexlessness becomes obligatory. The famous Council of Elvira, meeting in Spain in 305, decrees that all clerics "are ordered to abstain completely from their wives and not to have children." This Council does not deal with clerical celibacy, as many suppose, but with celibate clerical marriages.

When does this happen?

The process takes two centuries and is complete by the fourth century. The married head of household leadership in the Church of the first two centuries vanishes.

I do not suggest that some of the choices for celibacy during this period are not motivated by idealism and love. Nor that choices for marriage were always noble. The situation then was as it is now. I do suggest that the behavior and belief of the institutional Church in enforcing celibacy and defaming marriage were appalling.

"I have found where evil lives," Augustine cries out as the fourth century ends. "It lives in the genitals. See the place. *Ecce unde. Ecce unde.* See where the evil lives, in your body, in your sex organs, in your pleasure."

Is it naive for a married priest to ask: Where is Jesus Christ in all this? Where is the splendor of marriage and the miracle of children? Why has the glory of God's creation been dishonored and shamed?

We move forward now six centuries.

The psychological pressure to choose celibacy is enormous during the intervening centuries. The married priesthood continues, however, even though priests and their wives often are defamed, sometimes forcibly separated, always under suspicion.

There are, nonetheless, married popes late into the ninth century (Adrian II, who dies in 872, is married). Even after Lateran II in 1139 and the prohibition of marriage to all priests, there are married bishops throughout Europe. The major dioceses of England persist in choosing married bishops: Ely, London, Salisbury, Durham, Winchester. Law is viewed very differently in the twelfth century. Papal and conciliar prohibitions are considered position papers rather than legal regulations as we now understand them.

The contention that Church tradition never sanctioned marriage after ordination for priests is simply not true. Although this point may not be of interest to many people, it is important to mention it because it is the only argument, I believe, Rome has left in denying reinstatement.

Bishop R*ather of Verona, Italy, observes in the tenth century that priests arranged marriages for their daughters to other priests and that if he expelled all priests who live with women or who marry after ordination, there would be no one left (PL 136,491). Bishop Otto of Constance, Germany, gives permission for unmarried priests to marry (cf. Ranke-Heinemann). In 1076, Archbishop Lanfranc of Canterbury, England, forbids clerics to marry after ordination (implying that the practice was widespread) but he allows all priests already married to keep their wives, without distinguishing whether they married before or after ordination (cf. Barstow). The situation is fluid and bishops, in great numbers, apparently accept marriage after ordination. Rome, at this point, does not have the resources or, perhaps, the will to stop the practice. At a time when all marriage is considered a spiritual compromise, we cannot expect Church leaders to propose marriage after ordination. More telling is the fact that married men continue to be ordained in commanding numbers even though marriage is judged negatively. How much more fitting today is a married priesthood, when marriage is honored!

It should be clear that if Rome refuses reinstatement or a married priesthood, it is not because it is respecting tradition.

Let us move now to Ravenna, Italy. The year is 1007 and a baby, born to an impoverished mother of a large family is starving to death. The mother ignores the cries because the family does not have the means to raise him. A neighboring woman, ironically the wife of a married priest, saves the infant's life by begging the mother to nurse him. The child grows up to become a vicious adversary of married priests and their wives. This is Peter Damian. A century after he begins to preach, Second Lateran will terminate the married priesthood and the Church will order the break up of married priests' families.

A few portraits may give us insights into the climate of the late eleventh and early twelfth centuries as Church leaders tear out a tradition of married priesthood with roots in the New Testament.

In this final century of optional celibacy, Peter Damian brings to bear the psychological warfare begun by Origen and developed by Augustine. His intent is different from theirs; he seeks a law, a conciliar decree and papal support to end priests' marriages. Since all other measures have failed, force will be used.

Damian presents a classic argument on sex and ritual purity. He warns priests and their wives or whores as he calls them: "The hands that touch the body and blood of Christ must not touch the genitals of a whore." In a pitch of pathological hysteria, he sees women as "flesh of the devil," cause of our ruin, "the very stuff of sin," "pigs." Even Peter the Apostle does not escape censure: "Peter washed away the filth of his marriage with the blood of his martyrdom." Peter Damian, I might add, is a canonized saint of the Catholic Church.

In 1105, a young man, Serio of Bayeux, France, the son of a priest, is discharged from his benefice or inheritance because of a recent ruling of Pope Urban II. Priests' sons are forbidden the right to be ordained. The law seeks to deprive them of any inheritance they might have received from their fathers.

Serio defends himself with these startling observations.

The new law, he argues, denies the equality of all Christians conferred by Baptism. Ordination and law are utilized to make Christians unequal. To deny ordination to a man only because he is the son of a priest is punitive rather than pastoral, economic in its intent rather that evangelical.

He goes on to observe that the popes of the eleventh and twelfth century are obsessively committed to controlling the Church. Serio's point is well taken. Gregory VII, one of the most absolutist popes in Church history, declared a few decades before this, in 1075, that a pope can depose all princes since the pope alone rules both the temporal and the religious world. The unyielding character of Gregory VII dismayed his closest friends who found his sometimes single-minded fanaticism occasionally idealistic but often terrifying. Church history shows that the more autocratic the pope, the more rigid he is on obligatory celibacy.

The third point made by Serio is the most delicate. He charges that homosexual clergy are dominant and that they influence the movement to terminate the married priesthood.

Serio's comment appears accurate. John Boswell, professor of history at Yale, documents the record in his landmark book, *Christianity, Social Tolerance, and Homosexuality*. He demonstrates that the century from 1050-1150, the century of Peter Damian, Gregory VII, and Second Lateran, is a century in which homosexuality flourished in the clergy. Numerous commentators of the day complain about monasteries as homosexual centers; they raise questions about why severe laws are passed forbidding heterosexual relations in clerical marriages while no regulations are promulgated prohibiting homosexual relations in monasteries.

If the preponderance of homosexuals is true, the motive driving Second Lateran become all the more suspect. Monks had achieved great power and controlled the legislative centers of the Church at this time. Gregory VII was a monk and at least six other popes of the period. In citing this data, I do not wish to imply any judgmental attitude toward homosexuality.

As the twelfth century ends, a different Church emerges. It is a Church exclusively centered in the Western and Latin Rite, a Church in which the pope is supreme not only as bishop but as ruler of Europe. Canon Law assumes enormous importance and obligatory celibacy is a universal requirement for priests.

I suggest that obligatory celibacy requires a context similar to that of the twelfth century to prevail. The papacy must be seen as absolute and human sexuality must be considered an evil. Church law must become normative for Christian behavior and the world must be judged deficient and decadent. Since these conditions no longer exist or are even possible, obligatory celibacy cannot endure.

The more democratic a culture, the more imperative it is for Church leaders to explain obligations in ways people at large and priests in particular can understand and approve. The official Church can no longer do this. This is made patently clear in the extreme embarrassment and consistent reluctance of bishops to debate this issue in public. The world at large knows there is no convincing evidence to support the official position.

Obligatory celibacy is not beyond the capabilities of clergy and Catholics today; it is simply beyond their preferences. It is not preferred because it functions best in a medieval rather than in a modem world. Celibacy as an option is praiseworthy; as an obligation, it is an anachronism.

As Julian observed in his debate with Augustine, when marriage and women and sexuality are devalued, we are not arguing about the marital condition of a priest. We are raising questions about what we think of God and the Church and how we perceive family life and human freedom.

We are focused in this essay onredeeming humanity and what it is in us which needs redemption. We do not need to be redeemed from the world or from marriage, from women or from sexual experience, from freedom or from the signs of the times. Not a single one of these items is evil. All were made by God. We need only be redeemed from our misuse of these values and, especially, from the arrogance of imposing our will on others.

REDEEMING THE CHURCH FOR HUMANITY

We now know the main actors in the destruction of the married priesthood.

Who are they?

Origen and Augustine and Damian were major protagonists. Who today would want to defend obligatory celibacy with the arguments they used to enforce it? There were others, of course. Over so long a period of time, there had to be. Jerome and Crysostom, synods, and councils, homosexual clerics and sexually frightened heterosexuals, reforming popes and ambitious bishops, some saints and a few mystics, all played a part. The canvas is too vast to limit the scene to only the few we have named.

To Origen, Augustine and Damian, I would add two other major influences: Gregory VII and the Second Lateran Council.

A footnote might be in order. Many know that Second Lateran terminated the married priesthood in 1139. We are often less informed on the pope who called that Council. His name was Innocent II and his election was so notorious that it began an eight year schism. His predecessor died on February 13, 1130 and was hastily buried. In the middle of that night, a minority of cardinals elected him and staged an illegal coronation ceremony at daybreak of February 14. People met the new pope before knowing the former pope was dead and buried. A majority of cardinals called the election invalid and chose another pope. Innocent II's claims were reinforced by armies from England, Germany and France. The schism ended with the death of the antipope in 1138. Innocent and that Council terminate the married priesthood.

We asked above, who would want to defend obligatory celibacy with arguments from Origen, Augustine and Damian. We ask now, as we consider Gregory VII and Second Lateran, who would be able to find in the New Testament the Church they represented?

Why did this happen?

The married priesthood ended because of intense zeal for sexless lives by men who denigrated marriage, sexual experience and women. There were also questions of power and of property. Nor must we omit a defective sacramental theology which saw the Eucharist violated if celebrated by men committed to marital sexual love. Some were well intentioned and believed, no doubt, that God and Christ wished this, but even these despaired of human nature and the Holy Spirit and found violence acceptable. The preaching of Jesus about respect and love for one another and his efforts to persuade his disciples to choose values from internal conviction were scuttled so that the Kingdom of God might become the institutional Church.

When did this happen?

It happened in two stages. The second to the fourth centuries psychologically destroyed the respect for marriage, sex, and women. The eleventh and twelfth centuries destroyed the married priesthood and moved to create an imperial Church.

It may not be too much to declare that every theological and pastoral argument used by Rome to support obligatory celibacy has been discredited. The notion that married priests have violated their deepest commitments and promises is untrue. The Church we stand for is not a Church of Gregory VII and Second Lateran but the Church of Second Vatican and John XXIII. The Church we stand for is a Church that is not hostile to democracy, the modern world, American culture and the American Catholic Church. The Church we stand for is one in which married priests and their families and their brother bishops join together, as we did last year in Santa Clara, and pray for reconciliation so that we can support one another as we serve Christ and the world.

The past is best interpreted by its consequences in the long run. We did not know well what the voyages of Columbus meant until North and South America created the nations and cultures which came after him. We see Magna Carta in a different light after the American Constitution and the French Revolution.

Whatever the reasons for obligatory celibacy in the past, its consequences are hurting the Church now, wounding it greivously. The world at large and the Church as the whole body of Christ have opted for a reformed and renewed priesthood, a liberated and honest Church, a ministry and a community vastly different from that proposed by reactionary forces in Rome.

All the theoretical and theological work is complete. The studies have been compiled and published. The official Church position has lost in every instance. Obligatory celibacy is the option of an entrenched minority in power imposing it on an overwhelming majority that does not want it.

The issue, however, is much more than obligatory celibacy. The issue is God and the Church as a community. It is humanity and people as a family. It is women and their dignity as persons. We are really dealing with freedom and the Gospel, the celebration of creation and gratitude for our bodies. The subject is not sex. On its deepest levels, it has something to do with faith and how we are redeemed and whether that redemption is joyful and sensitive to our most profound needs as human beings and the essential integrity of our lives.

The time for talking and study may now have come to an end. We shall, of course, continue to dialogue with those who enforce the law and find Christ in it. We dialogue because we are, after all, Catholics. Many of us are priests and all of us are faithful to the Church in the mission Jesus Christ gave it.

We affirm the papacy and the bishops but also priests and laity. We support the need for law but also the claims of justice. We only wish to serve. Why does this threaten some Church leaders?

The Church we stand for does not endlessly debate an issue but concretely serves people's needs. It is time now to do this. We are clearly Catholics but, it should be obvious, we are not children. We give five sacraments to children; two are reserved for adults, marriage and ordination. Many of us have received both and all here have the fundamental right to be considered for both.

The Church we stand for is the Church we create now. There is no more time for fear and guilt and doubt and vengeance and accusations.

Who makes this Church happen?
We shall, you and I and all who join us.

Why shall we do this?
We shall do this from the conviction that God is with the Gospel and the Second Vatican Council and is with us now. We shall do this trusting that Christ will not lead us astray and will send us where we are needed.

When shall we do this?
We shall do this now. The time is *now*.

18

SETTING STANDARDS

Jesus has become an embarrassment for many church leaders and even for some theologians. The teaching of Jesus is appealed to as a rhetorical standard but the most credible standard for many in leadership today is "What does the pope wish?" "What did former popes say?" "What is written in the law?" and "What are the political realities of my taking a stand one way or the other?" None of this is wrong in itself, intrinsically evil, *intrinsice malum,* so to speak, but none of it is central.

Reform in the church cannot go very far unless it focuses on what Jesus said clearly. A reform which incorporates these values and gives them priority in ministry and church is the only authentic reform. This reform, I think, requires that we give witness to our faith, rather than merely deal with the politics of reform. The politics are not unworthy. Nonetheless, the deepest hunger in this community is spirituality and a longing for a church more closely aligned with Jesus. In this light, it might be helpful to focus on the parables of Jesus as the foundation for a new ecclesiology.

Two major church reformers come immediately to mind, both of them calling us back to the standards that Jesus set. One is Francis of Assisi. He hears a compelling voice cry out: "Francis, my church is in ruins." That line is uttered when the structured church is institutionally very powerful. Under Innocent III, the Roman Catholic Church reached the height of its power, and controlled, for all practical purposes, the entire known world. "Francis, my church is in ruins, because there is structure but so little spirit. Help me rebuild it."

Another great reformer, Martin Luther, observes in the sixteenth century: "If the structure of the church and the pope can do so much, then we do not need Jesus Christ any more." Karl Barth said it another way in the time before the Second Vatican Council when the Roman Catholic Church was powerfully in control, not of the world, but of its own internal life: "I hear the voice of Peter in that church, but where is the voice of Christ? Why does Peter have more to say than Christ? Is this how Peter would have wanted it to have gone?"

Jesus Christ has become an embarrassment for us.

I will divide this reflection into three sections. First I will talk about the parables as a basis for ministry to community. In the second part I will deal with ministry to the marginalized innocent. And, thirdly, I will talk about ministry to the marginalized guilty. I want to stay fairly close to the words of Jesus throughout.

MINISTRY TO COMMUNITY

There was once a man who had two sons. We all know the story. There are no coordinates in the landscape; the parable is psychological; it does not matter where it happened because it happens everywhere. It's cosmology is human. The man had two sons; they are not named; they are both teenagers; they are less than twenty. They had to be that young because under Jewish custom at the time of Jesus one had to be married by the age of 20 or else one could be brought to the court. They are siblings, of course.

There are so many sibling stories in Scripture: Cain and Abel, Esau and Jacob, James and John, Martha and Mary, the prodigal son and his brother.

The younger of the two brothers says to his father: "Give me my share of the estate. You are taking too long to die." So the man divided his property between them. It took the younger son a few days to gather all he had. The scene is dramatic. "So you are going," the father must have said. And the son, with embarrassed guilt and rebellious assertiveness, continues the task of gathering, while the father watches confused, ashamed, and filled with heartache. It is a cruel moment in that family's history. "My son will you go away, will you walk with me no more?"

The younger son does what many of us may do at moments in our lives, becoming prodigal and wasteful. He is a young man and all of a sudden he has a fortune. He travels to a distant country, and there he squanders his inheritance in dissolute living. When he had spent everything, a severe famine afflicted the country. Friendships fail when one loses power and money, and so the young man learns a bitter lesson. He is desperate for money for the first time, and hires himself to someone who sends him to feed pigs. At this point the young man has lost even his self-esteem. He grew up learning, as all Jews did, "cursed is the one who raises swine."

Jesus brilliantly depicts the scene of anguish and loss, perhaps because he observed it often in the lives of his contemporaries. The young man envies the swine their food. He feels hunger; he has no home and no friends, no family and no money, no self-esteem, not even survival skills, (because he was raised in a wealthy family), and he knows that all is his fault.

The contrast is astonishing. A moment before, he has money and is somebody. Then shortly after that he is fighting pigs for food and is aware that he is nobody, that no one cares for him or about him. In a few sentences, Jesus gives us a portrait of unbearable despair.

It is only in his wounds that the young man realizes for the first time the damage he has done to his father. The wounds of our lives are sometimes the first claim we have on compassion. But they may also be the first intimation of how we have wounded others. A theme that will occur in the citations that I give is Jesus' insistence that compassion is the hallmark for ministry.

The young man's salvation begins with his memories. When he is totally depleted, he remembers: "How many of my father's hired hands have bread enough to spare and I am dying of hunger. I will go back and I will say, Father, I have sinned. I know I was foolish, wasteful, destructive. Is there a chance you would let me come home, not as your son (I lost that) but as a slave or a worker?"

How often we have trained people in the church never to take others back. We leave the divorced and remarried without Communion until they die. Church administrators announce that they will never reconcile married priests and they declare this with pride. Some delight in the exclusion of homosexuals, dissidents, advocates of reproductive freedom. This parable rises up and accuses everyone who does not take people back, everyone who seeks vengeance when forgiveness alone will heal, everyone who asks that justice be done when only mercy will do. The most important thing a parent leaves a child, or a church can give its people, is the healing memory it leaves with them.

Memory now breaks through, and the son says: "I shall never be an orphan. All my life I will be part of my father's life. He would no more dismiss me than one member of my body would dismiss another member. My eye can never say to my hand, 'I have no need of you.' And so he will take me back. How do I know that? I know that because I know him, because he has left me with a memory of love. I know that he will not turn me away."

It must have been a thought such as this which brought Peter back to Christ, confessing: "O Master, I have failed. I have broken your heart. Could I walk with you again, not close as we once were, that may no longer be possible, but at least on the margin, not at the center where I once was, but at least at the edges." And Jesus says, "Peter, I love you. Do you love me?" "O Lord, you know that I love you."

So often in the church we do not hear the love because we have discounted the pain. We keep some people at a distance so great that we no longer see their faces or take note of the sound of their voices, their agony, their love.

When we write as we write now, there are those in the church who say, "But we must keep our standards. We cannot have reckless and naive forays into love and compassion." We need to answer: "But this is the standard we were given. We must insist less on what we need the other to do for us and more on what the other needs from us." This is ministry. This is truly ministry in the mind of Jesus. "I know my father will never turn against me," the prodigal son says. "He knows my heart is not bad even if my actions have been hurtful."

What memories does the church leave with us? Who in the church are we absolutely certain we could turn to when we are in need? That person is the church for us. That person is the vicar of Christ for our life. Whom would you turn to if everything were wounded in your life? If you had one person to seek out, would you seek out the pope, or the bishop, or the priest? Whom would you seek when you were unsteady, shaky, searching? Answer. And in your answer, you will truly know who the church is for you, and where Christ is to be found. Our most lasting ministry is the memories we leave with people. We know that we have failed in ministry when we hear someone say: "I didn't come back because I wasn't sure you would forgive me. I was not certain you would take me back. I was afraid you would hurt me more." When we feel unworthy on every level life, to whom would we turn? There is the church. The voice and the face of such a person is the voice of good shepherd and the face of Christ.

And so the young man says: "I will say, 'Father, be a father to me now when I need a father as I have never before needed a father. Father, I have sinned against heaven and I have hurt you. Don't make me an orphan by saying there is no place in your home or your heart for me. I have no right ever again to be at your table but find at least a crumb for me from the bread of life we once shared. I am not worthy. I have no claim on justice and yet, I ask you, take me back, give me a job, make me a slave." The young man asks that the father not forsake him. Not long after delivering this parable, the storyteller himself will pray a similar prayer from the cross.

Our church must not be a democracy. It must be more than that. It must be a community. In a community, such stories as this parable are possible and believable. But some church administrators object: "Such parables are naive and preposterous. They were for an earlier moment in the Church, but they work no more." How far we have come!

This parable measures the distance. How wrong a road we have taken in our prodigal search for orthodoxy and the right direction! Many in our Church have bartered our inheritance as a community for a bowl of porridge. We give up our identity as a community and home and become an institution and no more than that, a church in ruins, when we make this parable rhetoric rather than policy. We cannot close our ears to all the lost sons and daughters in our midst without becoming also deaf to Christ.

The story goes on. While the young man was still far off, the father saw him. I wish we could capture this moment on film: the face of the father, his eyes, the body language. It was a long wait. It took time for the young man to squander that much money. The father waited. "Will I die before I see my son again? How did I fail him as a father? Why did money mean more to him than my love?" The father had looked often down the road that took his son away. "My son was once there, why can't he be there again? Come back, my son, not only so that I can heal you, but so that you can forgive me for not having been more." And then Jesus says, "When he saw him," and this is the crucial line, "he was filled with compassion." The hallmark of ministry. The father does not yet know if the son has returned for forgiveness. He might be returning only for more money. No matter. The sight of the son is gift for the father. Sometimes, the presence of someone is all we want and more than we need.

The young man is frightened. It is the first time he has come near home and been frightened of his own home. Is this how some Catholics feel as they enter our churches? The son is determined. Love is a paradox of daring and diffidence. And so he continues. Then Jesus says "the father ran to him." The entire gospel and the entire church, can be summed up in that line. The father ran to him. The son seeing the father running to him knows that he is truly home. There are no words spoken. The father puts his arms around his son and kisses him as the son falls into his father's arms like a shipwrecked mariner.

Then the speech which all of a sudden is not as necessary or as difficult to deliver as it once seemed to be: "Father, I have hurt you. I am not worthy to be called your son. Don't hurt me, don't hate me, don't turn me away. If you will not give me life or take me in, where can I go?" The young man speaks the language of defeat, the language we all speak when our resources are depleted. All that the father hears is the first word: Father. No other word matters. The father answers with a liturgy. He vests his son with symbols of celebration and acceptance. "You are not a slave. This is my son," he says to the servant. "Bring him not the work clothes of a slave, but the best robe we have, not the yoke of submission, but a ring on his finger, not bare feet but sandals." A son, never a slave, wears robes and rings and sandals.

The liturgy of the Word, so to speak, ends here as syllables and symbols and vestments bring us to the breaking of the bread.

The father moves from compassion to communion, ready to offer the bread of life, not the crumbs of sterility. Jesus once asked what kind of a father would give a son a stone when he came for bread? The communion table, you see, is for those who need it most. What could possibly have led us to put in our missalettes and in our law that nonCatholics must not approach our table to receive communion?

Could we have made such rules in a Church built on parables?

We know of course the story of the elder son. He is angry. He is bitter. He is part of the communion police. Law over sacrament. Filled with anger, he is a harsh official, rather than a son of the same father. He makes a brilliant case for vengeance. It is often easier to make a case for vengeance than for forgiveness. Contrast the way each brother addresses the father. "Look, you," the angry son cries. The younger son had said, "Father." Then the elder son tells us where he really is, where so many in the Church still are: "I have slaved for you all my fife." The younger son had pleaded, "Take me home." "I never disobeyed your orders," the older son continues. Note the words, "your orders." The older son has built a life on obedience, feeling uncomfortable with love and forgiveness.

The self-righteous lawgiver makes obedience the highest norm. What happens to a church when allegiance to the pope's orders is the basic reason for ministry? "I never disobeyed your orders." Ironically it is the older son who is the slave in that home, not because the father wishes it but because the older son perceives life this way. The elder son shouts out in anger, "but this son of yours...." He says in effect what so many Catholics unfortunately can say: "I don't want to be part of a family that forgives. If there is amnesty for married priests and for the divorced and remarried, I don't want to be part of that family. I would rather be bitter like the elder brother, and I wish to be that because I hate my life and I hate everything that I have been forced to do in it." Such a small Church! Such piteously diminished spirits! Hearts of stone!

The real prodigal is the elder son who has wasted his entire life. All that the younger son wasted was money. The elder son attacks the father, never using the term "father."

There is always a peril in forgiving. We may become the victim of the anger of those whose lives are filled with rage and resentment.

The elder son's smallness contrasts with the father's generosity. "My son," he says, "all I have is yours." The father had come out of the house to plead with the elder son. Going out to the son is against Jewish custom; yet the father does this for both sons. The father makes a desperate effort to bring his first son to love. "Your brother was lost, I can't afford to lose him again." The parable reminds us that we cannot hold a family or a community together with justice. Justice is for strangers and institutions. Justice is what a community settles for it has lost its heart. Love finds justice deficient and confining. Love prepares a feast while justice counts the calories.

Let me end this first section with one other image of ministry from the Gospels. Jesus got up from the table, took off his outer robe, tied a towel around himself, poured water into a basin, and began to wash his disciples' feet and to wipe them with the towel that was tied around him. John, of course, as we are well aware, is the only evangelist who does not give us the breaking of the bread at the Last Supper. The sacrament of the Last Supper for him is service and ministry raised to the highest standard in the washing of the feet. The disciples were astonished because Jesus at this moment takes on the social role of a woman and a slave. Only women and slaves washed people's feet.

Jesus comes to Simon Peter: "Lord, are you going to wash my feet?" Jesus observes, "You don't know what I am doing, but later you will understand." Peter counters, "You will never wash my feet, never, never; you will never wash my feet." Then Jesus said, "Peter, if I do not wash your feet, you cannot be part of me." And Peter said, "Lord, my hands and my head as well." A powerful moment between Peter and Christ. After he washed their feet, he put his robe on, returned to the table and said, "Do you know what I have just done for you? You call me Teacher and Lord, and that is what I am. If I, the Lord, have washed your feet, you must do this for one another."

In Matthew, Jesus observed: "If your son asks for bread, do you give him a stone? If your daughter asks for a fish, do you give her a snake? You know how the irreligious lord it over others and how their leaders are always conscious of who has authority and who does not. It must never be that way with you. Never!"

Jesus then continues, "I will not leave you orphans. This is my commandment, that you love one another as I have just loved you."

It is so simple. How did we miss it? "I do not call you slaves or servants."

The parable of the prodigal son is the echo of all this teaching. "I have called you friends. You are my friends."

What kind of a man would think of the parable we have just heard or would do what he did in the washing of the feet? What would have entered into his mind to do such things? What a magnificent heart he had! What kind of a church should have come from this? How did we get it wrong? Why did we get it wrong? Why don't we make it right now?

MINISTRY TO THE MARGINALIZED INNOCENT

Ministry to the self and to the community is the fundamental ministry.

The second level of ministry that emerges from the parables is ministry to the marginalized innocent. What I would like to consider in this regard is the parable of the good Samaritan. Jesus again contrasts law with compassion.

A lawyer stood up to test him, "Teacher, what must I do to inherit eternal life?" Jesus says, "What's in the law?" And the lawyer says, "You will love the Lord, your God, with all your heart and soul and strength and mind, and your neighbor as yourself." Then Jesus, moving him from orthodoxy to orthopractice, says, "You've given the right answer. Do this and you will live." The lawyer is embarrassed because the answer is too simple. He wants something more complicated: "Who is my neighbor?" Jesus then tells the story of the Good Samaritan. To give it context, there are some things we should know.

It is twenty-three miles from Jerusalem to Jericho, a long and perilous journey. Jerusalem is 2,250 feet above sea level, Jericho is nine hundred feet below sea level. For this reason, one goes "down" to Jericho even though Jericho is north of Jerusalem. Wealthy people live in Jericho, most of the priests, unfortunately. The road, therefore, was filled with robbers and was dangerous. Travel in the ancient world was always risky.

A man fell into the hands of robbers. They stripped him, they beat him and they left him to die. The first person who comes down the road after the assault is a priest. He sees the man and passes to the other side of the road; partly because victims are an inconvenience, partly because legal impurity could happen if a priest touches a bleeding body. In the action of the priest we see the God whom that priest worshipped was a God of laws rather than a God of life. There is always a good reason to pass by, especially in the ancient world when one never traveled for frivolous reasons.

Then a levite passed by. A levite would be a temple official, clergy. He too passes on the other side.

One might imagine the lawyer was becoming uncomfortable at this point. Many of his connections in Jerusalem were with priests and levites and they are not being presented favorably in this parable. Then a Samaritan comes by with good reasons to ignore the dying man: *religious reasons* - this man who is dying is a heretic; *social reasons* - a Samaritan does not deal with a Jew; *historical reasons* - Samaritans and Jews have plundered each other's lives and homes; *psychological reasons* - the Samaritan is traveling on urgent business; and *personal reasons* - *it* is a messy situation and one that may not be appreciated by the person one assists.

Jesus is disturbing his audience by making a Samaritan the hero of the story. The Samaritan approaches the dying man. He is filled with compassion. One traveled in the ancient world with a first–aid kit consisting of wine and oil: wine, an antiseptic and oil, a curative. The Samaritan responds very concretely to the victim: wine and oil, then bandages. He picks the man up, holds him in his arms, puts him on a donkey, and brings him to an inn. This time there is room in an inn. The God of Israel, in effect, Jesus is saying, is a God of mercy. The Samaritan takes out two denarii, about a hundred dollars, and also leaves an open account. "Take care of him and when I come back I'll pay all the costs."

As the story ends, Jesus turns the table and asks the lawyer, "Which of the three is the neighbor? Which one is the minister: the priest, the temple official, or the one we have been taught to despise? Which of the three is the neighbor?" How different questions sound when we make them concrete! Let us try concrete questions in terms of problems in today's Church. Why can't my father celebrate liturgy publicly anymore? Because he had me as a son? Why can't my sister celebrate liturgy? Because she is a woman. But she loves God and people. Is my homosexual brother intrinsically evil in his actions? Then why don't I feel the evil around him? Why is it when I'm near him I can only sense the fact that he loves? Is my mother less a woman because she found love only in her second marriage? We make such cruel distinctions in the church, especially when we make the legal standard more demanding than the existential situation. Do we not often say to priests: In pastoral life and in secret you may always be compassionate, but be compassionate only selectively in pubic? Compassion ruins your career and you will embarrass the Church. If you must be compassionate controversially, do it behind closed doors in the internal forum, in the confessional, on a deathbed. Jesus forgave recklessly, openly. Should not this be our standard?

The lawyer who chooses not to say the word Samaritan, he hates it so much, finally gives the right answer, "The one who had compassion, the one who had pity in his heart." Jesus says, "You've got it. That's right."

When that young Jewish man beaten on the open road woke up a few days later he must have been changed forever. "Who brought me here? How did I get here?" As he heard the story, he must have been profoundly moved.

He could never, after this, teach his children, as he was once taught, to hate Samaritans. And so the healing is spiritual as well. Why is it we do not take greater risks for compassion?

What makes us use the name of Jesus to justify what Jesus would never, could never do?

MINISTRY TO THE MARGINALIZED GUILTY

The woman has no name. She is known only by her crime or her sin. It is always that way when we are ready to execute people. We refer to them by their crime or their sin. Their name does not matter. She is a woman, which already means she is of little account socially. She is an adulteress and that, of course, does not help.

Notice what Jesus does in these parables and actions: he tells us about a son who did not obey and he rescues him; about a Samaritan who was rejected by the institution and he exalts him. He washes people's feet which is what a free Jewish man was told he must never do. The common thread, in every instance, is compassion over law.

The woman will be used to make a point. Women frequently are used to make a point. She is to be executed for adultery. There is an incredible intersection here between authority, sex and property The Jewish community linked adultery with property rather than with sex. This is why, under Jewish law, if a single Jewish woman had sex with a married man, it was not adultery because she was not property. But if a single man had sex with a married Jewish woman, it was adultery because she was someone else's property. In any case the death of this woman will be an irrelevance.

The great fear of so many people about the Church is that if we are compassionate this will create license. Some would look at the prodigal son and say, "If we let the son get away with that, a third of his father's estate, family life will disintegrate." The woman taken in adultery, "If we let women get away with that, marriage will disintegrate." With the Samaritan, "If people know that ministry happens outside our system, especially with those to whom ministry is forbidden, the church will disintegrate." There are large groups of people in our church who seem to be preoccupied with disintegration.

This story is filled with the language of power and law. What it says is that sometimes a woman's death is necessary so that the system can work. If she dies, it's a price worth paying for order in the system. Today we say that order in the Church is important, and we are willing to pay a high price in human lives and human happiness in order to keep the system working. If people no longer have the gospel preached or get pastoral care, it is a small price to pay, some suppose, so that the system will work in the way we prefer. At some point, however, the price for order is the loss of order and the whole community is left in disarray. At times the price we pay for order is giving up love and honesty and even the Gospel.

I have always been intrigued by the fact that Matthew, Mark and John begin the passion story with a woman performing an anointing. Luke does not, although he is the one who emphasized the role of women in his gospel. We find this story of the woman in adultery in the eighth chapter of John, but scripture scholars agree that the Greek in this passage is Luke's and that it belongs at the end of chapter 21 or the beginning of chapter 22. This is where Luke begins the passion narrative. It is a powerful introduction!

It is early in the morning as this story unfolds. Jesus comes to the temple, the symbol of institutional authority. Jesus is in Jerusalem. He seems more comfortable in rural settings which is why his parables are set in the country side. People come to him and he begins to teach.

The scribes and pharisees bring in a woman who had just been caught in adultery. Jesus knows their faces. He knows they are hostile. He is in Jerusalem. He is at the temple, and he is soon surrounded by enemies. The accusers make the woman, marked for death, stand before all of them. "Teacher, this woman was caught in the act of committing adultery." The woman is being used, degraded by being forced to stand there, treated as an object.

Jewish law was savage. An adulterous woman must be stoned to death immediately. That would have happened to Mary had Joseph decided to press charges. Every Jewish woman knew that. This Jewish woman knew that. It was written in Leviticus and Deuteronomy and women were told this from their earliest years. It will not be the last time when religious people will suppose that violence may be pleasing to God.

They said all of this, of course, so that they might have charge to bring against him. So the woman is only a means to an end. Jesus bent down and wrote with his finger on the ground, and then he delivered a haunting line. "If there is someone who has never committed a sin, let that person begin the execution." He continues writing on the ground. Embarrassed, they start to walk away, slowly, in order, reluctantly. Jesus was left alone with the woman standing before him. "Woman, is there no one left to condemn you?" The only time she speaks, "There is … there is no one." "Nor will I condemn you." I don't know if she had seen Jesus before, but even if she had, she sees him differently now, because the face of the deliverer always looks different in the act of deliverance.

CONCLUSION

We have heard stories of a lost son in one parable, of a lost daughter in the woman caught in adultery, of a Samaritan who saved a dying Jew, and of a Christ who washed the feet of his disciples. The common thread is that ministry is defined by the need others have of us.

What are the needs today? Not more rules, I believe. Just imagine if the rules were followed in the parables and actions of Jesus: the prodigal son would have been sent away, the woman in adultery would have been killed, the Samaritan would have left the man alone to die, and the washing of feet could not have been done by Jesus because a male who was free could not do this.

Don't we see what Jesus is trying to say about ministry and church? Why is it we have eyes to see and do not see? Who gives us the right to withhold healing and to do this in the name of Christ? How can we fit the Church into these parables, especially when Church policy is identified with the wrong characters in the parables? Church policy is, too often, the elder brother, angry, demanding obedience and vengeance. Church policy is the Jewish priest on the open road rather than the good Samaritan. Does anyone know a Catholic priest who was ever dismissed from ministry for not being compassionate? Church policy is the executioner of women keeping them in their place, especially punishing women when the offenses are sexual.

Jesus is such an embarrassment. One of the most beautiful things that has happened to us since Vatican II is that you and I have started to believe, as we never did before, in a church of love rather than a church of law. A church, therefore, that makes more of obedience than compassion, which withholds forgiveness and reconciliation and prefers to punish the prodigal son, which no longer sees the victims of its own policies on the open roads of life and which passes to the other side rather than to minister to their needs, which picks up stones to keep women on the margins, which insists on the law excluding women from the sanctuary, which does not value women for their needs and gifts, such a church has stopped being the church of Christ. A church which silences all its prophets is a church which would crucify Jesus again.

Jesus is an embarrassment for those who find comfort in institution and law. They place their security in those they see: the pope or bishops or pastors. "Blessed are those who have not seen and still believe."

What we have done, unfortunately, in acting against these parables, is to have built temples of exclusion and oppression, introduced the slavery of law and brought back sacrifice, not of animals, but of people's self-worth, believing that God would be glorified in their destruction.

The parables remain outside the temple and there we find Christ. God, after all, sent us Christ, not a church. We shall not find our way again until faith in Christ is more visible than our faith in church.

A true Christian creed should now confess: It was always you, gracious God, whom we sought. You were the mother and the father we longed for and never found, the son we embraced coming back to us after so much longing for his return. It was always you, gracious God, you were the healer who came to us as we were wounded and neglected on the open roads of life. You were the deliverer, the unexpected stranger, who gave us compassion. You were the one who took us in your arms when no one else would, who lifted us up from the dirt and the danger where we were beaten. It was always you. You were the one who poured water in a basin and came and washed our feet. It was always you. Remember us when you enter into paradise. Do not leave us behind at the door as our Church can do so easily, not counting the cost or the pain it inflicts. We can only be safe in the Church, if we are first safe in you, because it is only you who is infallible, never failing, always renewing. It was always you, was it not? This is the great truth we have learned on our journey of life. We ask you now to bring us home, to put rings on our fingers and sandals on our feet, and hold us. It was always you. Call us your sons and daughters once more and let us call you father and mother once again. Bring us to your table where in the breaking of the bread we will recognize you. Then send us out as ministers of compassion to a world whose heart is broken. Wash our feet so that we shall never forget your commandment of love. When our task is done, bring us home and tell us that we were worthy and let us know we did some good and even show us the faces of those we healed. Then we shall have found the church, for in finding you we find the church and in losing you we lose everything. It was always you, gracious God. You have called us by name, and in hearing our name, we have found, in your voice, a Shepherd, a Savior, and the Church of Christ.